PRAISE FOR
HOW WE RELATE

How We Relate will help you understand your personality traits and why you're inclined in the ways you are. But that's not really what it's about. This book is about connection—about helping you discover what you've never noticed in yourself or in others so that you can relate, commune, serve, and love. That is the kind of help I need, and you probably do too.

RUSSELL MOORE, editor-in-chief, *Christianity Today*

The Enneagram is a profoundly helpful tool for self-discovery. But what do we do *after* we've dissected our own personalities and then have to put on shoes, walk out the door, and interact with a diverse world? Jesse Eubanks helps us answer that question, and more, through this insightful resource.

A. J. SHERRILL, Anglican priest and author of *Being with God: The Absurdity, Necessity, and Neurology of Contemplative Prayer*

Relationships matter, and they can bring us the greatest joys and cause us the deepest hurts. So becoming aware of how and why we relate to others in certain ways is extremely important for our well-being. Jesse Eubanks has given us a clear and practical guide on how to access the tool of the Enneagram within a Jesus-centered context to understand ourselves and to nurture strong and life-giving relationships. What a gift!

MARILYN VANCIL, author of *Self to Lose, Self to Find: Using the Enneagram to Uncover Your True, God-Gifted Self*

How We Relate guides readers to Jesus and his radiant gospel as they discover their wirings through the Enneagram. With honesty, wit, and wisdom, Jesse Eubanks offers one of the most helpful resources on the subject to help Christians navigate how they relate.

DR. JAMAAL WILLIAMS, lead pastor, Sojourn Church Midtown, Louisville, Kentucky

"The purpose of life is relationships," writes Jesse Eubanks in *How We Relate*. Through a thoughtful exploration of the Enneagram, the gospel, and his own story, Jesse masterfully interweaves these threads together to create a powerful chord of interconnectedness between an awareness of self and others. He helps readers pay attention to the things that matter—things of the soul and lives lived well, loving others and ourselves, from our *true* selves.

PAUL ANGONE, author of *Listen To Your Day:*
The Life-Changing Practice of Paying Attention

Knowing the Enneagram and how your personality is structured is a gift, which can truly be useful only after you've discovered how your Enneagram type helps and hurts you. Each of us is a gift to the world—one that can be beautiful only when we embrace all of who we are and who our friends, neighbors, coworkers, and families are. *How We Relate* is a practical and valuable guide to receiving what is beautiful and rejecting what is false about who God created you to be.

SEAN PALMER, author of *Speaking by the Numbers: Enneagram Wisdom for*
Pastors, Teachers, and Communicators and *Forty Days on Being a Three*

How We Relate moves the Enneagram beyond self-awareness and into the context of relationships. When used solely for self-reflection, the Enneagram falls short of its full value because we were created for connection. In these pages, Jesse Eubanks will help you discover that a truly meaningful life is found in your everyday relationships with God and others.

BETH AND JEFF MCCORD, founders of Your Enneagram Coach

JESSE EUBANKS

HOW WE

RELATE

Understanding God, Yourself,
and Others through
THE ENNEAGRAM

ZONDERVAN
BOOKS

ZONDERVAN BOOKS

How We Relate
Copyright © 2023 by Jesse Eubanks

Requests for information should be addressed to:
Zondervan, *3900 Sparks Dr. SE, Grand Rapids, Michigan 49546*

Zondervan titles may be purchased in bulk for educational, business, fundraising, or sales promotional use. For information, please email SpecialMarkets@Zondervan.com.

ISBN 978-0-310-36522-8 (audio)

Library of Congress Cataloging-in-Publication Data

Names: Eubanks, Jesse, 1979, author.
Title: How we relate : understanding God, yourself, and others through the Enneagram / Jesse Eubanks.
Description: Grand Rapids : Zondervan, 2023. | Summary: "How can we share ourselves if we don't know ourselves? In How We Relate, Enneagram coach and host of The EnneaCast podcast Jesse Eubanks invites you to discover who you are by interacting with the Enneagram through the gospel story to grow in your self-awareness, improve your relationships, and encounter Jesus."—Provided by publisher.
Identifiers: LCCN 2022031551 (print) | LCCN 2022031552 (ebook) | ISBN 9780310365198 (hardcover) | ISBN 9780310365211 (ebook)
Subjects: LCSH: Interpersonal relations—Religious aspects—Christianity. | Enneagram. | Typology (Psychology)—Religious aspects—Christianity. | BISAC: PSYCHOLOGY / Personality | RELIGION / Christian Living / Spiritual Growth
Classification: LCC BV4597.52 .E925 2023 (print) | LCC BV4597.52 (ebook) | DDC 158.2—dc23/eng/20220906
LC record available at https://lccn.loc.gov/2022031551
LC ebook record available at https://lccn.loc.gov/2022031552

Published in association with the literary agent Don Gates @ THE GATES GROUP, www.the-gates-group.com.

Cover design: Faceout Studio / Tim Green
Cover illustration: beastfromeast / iStock
Interior illustrations: Jesse Eubanks
Interior design: Denise Froehlich

Printed in the United States of America

---

22 23 24 25 26 27 28 29 30 31 32 /LSC/ 15 14 13 12 11 10 9 8 7 6 5 4 3 2 1

For Lindsay My Beautiful—
thank you for showing me
how to love and be loved.
And for imagining the first doodles
that eventually created this book.

CONTENTS

THE HEAD TRIAD

How We Relate Is How We Relate

⎯⎯⎯⎯●⎯⎯⎯⎯

If you want a meaningful life,
invest in your relationships.

Years ago, I was sitting in a circle of chairs with about a dozen other men. We were in a cold room on the third floor of an old elementary school that had been turned into a church. It was the edge of springtime and gloomy outside. The leader was encouraging us to each share a burden we had been carrying for a long time and couldn't seem to get past. Sitting with a small group of people talking about their burdens can be excruciating, but he said doing so takes the shame away because we see that others aren't judging us. (Oh, if only they knew the firing squad I had stationed at the ready in my head.)

As each man shared, I foolishly assumed I could pinpoint their issue within the first sixty seconds. One guy felt insecure at work and wasn't sure what to do about a coworker. (Problem: He was insecure. Solution: Be more confident.) One guy was having marriage problems. (Problem: He had anger issues. Solution: Stop yelling at your wife.) One guy was wealthy and wanted to use his money wisely to help people. (Problem: You're rich. Solution: I'm not. You have the power to fix that.)

When it finally circled around to me, I suddenly felt hazy. It was like fog had filled my head, and I could only make out vague shadows and abstracts of light. All clarity was gone. I started fumbling around in the dark, trying to explain my problem. I rambled about how ministry hadn't been going well for a long time, how my neighbors didn't seem interested in me, how I had sacrificed for God but he wasn't doing much with that sacrifice. As I spoke, I became more animated and emotive. I don't really remember what I said over the next fifteen minutes, but I do remember the recoiled silence in the room when I concluded my sharing time by yelling, ". . . and that's why I'm mad at God!" (As I once heard someone say, "Sometimes anger is how the truth escapes jail.")

I was as shocked as anyone else. Until that moment, I had no idea I was so resentful. I honestly thought of myself as pretty easygoing, hopeful, and in tune with my emotions. I suddenly realized I had been avoiding the truth. The ideas I had about myself were not consistent with who I really was. I was resentful toward God. I was also resentful toward others and especially toward myself. The gap between my dreams of how life could be and the reality I was trapped in had grown bigger than I could hold. My grip was slipping, and the scariest thing was that I had no idea it was happening.

Have you ever experienced this? Are you able to see the problems and solutions of others with clarity but suffer from blindness when it comes to yourself?

Self-clarity is difficult to obtain and not for the faint of heart. Moving beyond the surface level and into the recesses of our soul is a terrifying journey. We are scared of what we will find and scared of

"MAYBE I'M NOT SEEING EVERYTHING?"

who or what might be down there. Jesus tells us that knowing him and walking with him will lead to truth, and that truth will set us free (John 8:31–32). However, we believe if we discover the truth about ourselves, we'll be swallowed by shame and humiliation. To desire self-clarity is to risk seeing ourselves, not for who we want to

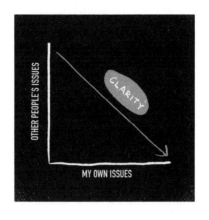

be, but for who we really are. It's easier to stay asleep to the truth. Self-clarity wakes us up.

At the time I was sitting in that cold room on the third floor, other areas of my life weren't going well either. My marriage was unhappy. I was consistently overwhelmed and aggravated as a new parent. The nonprofit where I worked was on the verge of bankruptcy. To top it off, our ministry staff spent days publicly telling people about the love of Jesus while privately bickering and mistrusting each other. I was burned-out, and my relationship with God was on autopilot. Relational trust and intimacy were at an all-time low in my life.

But I wasn't the only one who was affected. My wife felt unsupported by me. My kids felt nervous around me because of my temper. My coworkers felt frustrated by my incessant need to reinvent the wheel and innovate, even when it wasn't necessary. And I was blind to all of it. I saw everyone else as the problem. But as it turns out, I was playing a much bigger role than I wanted to admit.

· · ●●●●· ··

There is a question that humanity has been wrestling with since the dawn of time: "What is the purpose of life?" If I could be so

THE PURPOSE OF LIFE IS RELATIONSHIPS.

bold, I would like to humbly submit my answer:

The purpose of life is relationships.

The phrase "one another" occurs one hundred times in the New Testament. Almost sixty of those occurrences are commands about how we relate to one another. Examples from this lengthy list include callings to "love one another," "be devoted to one another," and "care for one another."

In other words, God's great desire for you is to love and be loved.

However, we have a problem—a relational problem. Let me illustrate: What do you think is the number one cause of missionaries leaving the field?

If you're like me, you likely assume it's due to issues like persecution, lack of funding, or even illness. As it turns out, none of those are correct. The number one reason Christians leave the mission field is conflict with other Christians.[1]

That's right. Sometimes even spiritual superheroes want to break someone's nose. But this isn't just a problem in the mission field. I'd venture to say this is also the reason Christians leave marriages, leave churches, and leave friendships. Often, the problem is not the world; the problem is us.

We don't know how to do relationships.

This is especially tragic for us as Christians because if you ask anyone with basic Bible knowledge, they'll tell you that the Scriptures can be summarized by Jesus' words in the gospel of Matthew: Love the Lord your God, and love your neighbor as yourself.

Jesus tells us that all of life is about loving and being loved in relationships.

Richard Rohr once wrote, "How we relate to God always reveals how we will relate to people, and how we relate to people is an almost infallible indicator of how we relate to God and let God relate to us. The whole Bible is a school of relationship."[2]

Did you catch that? How we relate *is* how we relate.

Each of us has a relational style—our one way we approach doing relationships—and we apply it to everyone, even God. This is why Scripture tells us we can't love God if we don't love others and that when we love others we also love God (Matthew 25:31–46; 1 John 4:7–8). It's why we're told in Mark 12 to "love your neighbor as yourself" (v. 31). How we relate is how we relate.

This is why understanding our style of relating is critical.

• • • ● ● ● • • •

Sitting in that cold room, I looked around and realized I *needed* better relationships. I was desperate. I was willing to do whatever was necessary. So I started going to counseling and found some guys to meet with on a weekly basis where I could practice vulnerability and receiving feedback.

One of the awful things I had

WE THINK OUR SELF-DECEPTION ONLY HURTS US.

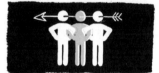

FALSE.

to face about myself was my own lack of self-awareness. I hadn't been able to see how my style of relating to others was impacting my life. I quickly learned that being oblivious about myself made it harder for me to have robust relationships. As hard as I tried, I simply didn't have the tools for the level of self-clarity or empathy that others needed from me. It was at this low point in my life that my counselor introduced me to a tool that helped me grow closer to God and others, and to even be less afraid of the truth about myself. It was a tool called the Enneagram.

The Enneagram

The Enneagram is a system of personality typing that describes patterns in how people perceive, process and present.[3] The basic idea is that our personalities are composed of our emotions, thoughts, and actions. *Ennea* means "nine," and *gram* means "points." There are nine different personality types—each driven by a different desire. These desires are so powerful that they forge our personality and distinguish one personality type from another. The Enneagram attempts to map all of this in a way that is easy to understand while resisting the temptation to reduce people into caricatures.

PERCEIVE + PROCESS + PRESENT

Unlike other personality systems that box people into a rigid framework, the Enneagram looks at a wide array of traits that go into our personalities. Each person has a *core type*—a primary center that drives them. However, we each pull in traits from the other types as well. Imagine your core type as your favorite black coffee. The characteristics you pull in from the other types are the creamers that give your drink the specific taste you prefer. Each person is a unique mixture of all nine types. No two personalities are identical.

How does this help with the problem of our relationships? The Enneagram allows us to see that everyone has different ways of perceiving, processing, and presenting. Understanding that each of us is driven by different core needs improves our empathy so that we don't assume people are intentionally hurting us or trying to drive us crazy.

The origins of the Enneagram are mysterious and often contested. Some say it came from the early church in the fourth century. Others say it was primarily developed in the last hundred years.

It's not really clear, but what is clear is that, with such a broad list of contributors (both Christian and not), the Enneagram is best understood not as a 'Christian' tool but as a human tool.[4] Like economics, medicine, or astronomy, the category is neutral. What we do within that category determines how compatible it is with Christian faith. I'm grateful for the tool of the Enneagram and how it has helped me in my relationship with God, others, and myself.[5]

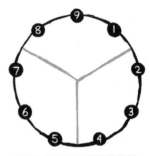

THIS IS A VERSION OF THE ENNEAGRAM. 9 TYPES IN 3 TRIADS IN 1 CIRCLE.

Since my days of yelling about God to other men in an old elementary school, I have become an Enneagram coach. I've spent years reflecting on the Enneagram— teaching workshops, hosting *The EnneaCast* (a podcast about the Enneagram), interviewing some of the best authors and teachers available, and doing private coaching. From my own life, as well as from the lives I've walked with, I'm convinced the Enneagram can be a useful tool that God uses to show us a path toward better relationships.

Many people have used the Enneagram purely for diagnostic purposes without engaging the call to transformation. It's important to understand that the Enneagram is not an excuse for poor conduct. ("I'm not bullying them—I'm just an Eight" or "I'm not overreacting—I'm just a Four.") If a diagnosis reveals we are sick, it is our responsibility to pursue a treatment plan, not revel in our illness. Nor is the Enneagram meant to reduce people to simply a type. In fact, we have qualities from all nine types to greater or lesser degrees. *When used well, the Enneagram allows for the complexity of humanity and enables transformation.* It's because of this that I hope to offer three distinct contributions to the Enneagram.

The Enneagram Needs Your Story

It is impossible to understand your Enneagram profile apart from your life story. In fact, your Enneagram can only be interpreted *through* your life story. Like all great stories, each chapter of your life has built on the one that came before it—leading you to where you are now. If you have only the Enneagram, you have only half the equation. We need both to have self-clarity. This is why I often say "Enneagram + Life Story = Clarity."

I have arranged the content of this book in a narrative structure:

- beginning with childhood;
- then exploring the nurturing of your False Self (more on this later);
- then reflecting on your encounter with Jesus; and
- culminating in the redemption of your True Self (more on this too).

This structure may at first glance seem to oversimplify the complexities of life, but seeing your life clearly as a narrative is helpful. I like a good, exciting story and want to give yours the arc it deserves.

The Enneagram Needs Jesus

The Enneagram cannot save you. It has no magical powers and no relational interest in you. The Enneagram cannot love you into wholeness. However, there is someone who can.

I've been on the edge of faith more times than I can count, but the person who always brings me back is Jesus. I have never met anyone more thrilling, beautiful, strong, or merciful than Jesus. He is too dynamic to be an invention and too wonderful to be just a man.

WE WORSHIP THE GOD WHO EMPATHIZES.

In this book, we'll explore two specific aspects of Jesus—his empathy and his authority. Why? We give our trust to someone when we believe they truly understand our problems *and* they have shown a mastery of how to overcome those problems. In other words, "Empathy + Authority = Trust." One of the marvels of Christian faith is the belief that God understands and shares our pain. We worship the God who empathizes. If this is true, then Jesus empathizes with each of the nine types. Does he stop merely at empathy? No. We'll also explore how Jesus models his mastery of personality and why he commands our attention. I am convinced that when we recognize that Jesus understands our pain and also recognize his demonstration of authority over our lives, we will give him our trust and foster a deeper and even more life-changing relationship with him (and others).

The Enneagram Needs the Gospel

Pastor and theologian Tim Keller says, "The Gospel is good news not good advice."[6] Traditional Enneagram teachers instruct that being virtuous leads to a happier life (works produce salvation).

Christian faith teaches that good news—the gospel of Jesus—frees us to become virtuous (salvation produces works). I am far more interested in giving you *good news*. If we do not recognize the

WHAT WE REALLY NEED IS GOOD ~~ADVICE~~ NEWS

good news that Jesus has for us, we may accidentally think we are free, while in reality we have replaced one set of chains for another.

What is this good news? It is the news that your wounds can be healed and your sins forgiven. Every parent knows that each of their children requires a unique approach and that love takes a different shape for each child. In the same way, I believe that God has a special message for you based on your personality. The gospel of Jesus is a diamond—a multifaceted collection of good news with diverse personal and social implications. While all nine types need the entirety of the gospel, I suspect that different angles of this diamond will pierce each of our hearts in a remarkable and touching way. God customizes his love for you.

What Do You Want?

If the purpose of life is relationships—to love God and love others—why wouldn't you want to keep growing? You're putting your relationships at risk if you stay where you are. If you stay here, you're like I was in that small group years ago, surprised by my anger at God and my distance from others. You're in danger of continuing to misunderstand others and be misunderstood yourself. You run the risk of missing out on seeing God's customized love for you and embracing more of the abundant life he is offering.

STOP GAMBLING YOUR RELATIONSHIPS.

LET'S LEARN TO DO BETTER.

God worked through the Enneagram to bring healing and flourishing to my relationships. I believe the Enneagram can change your life just as much as it has changed mine.

To feel loved, you must be known. To be known, you must share yourself. To share yourself, you must know yourself.

Come and see who you are.

CHAPTER 1

CREATED FOR
COMMUNITY

*The soul expresses itself as personality.
Personality expresses itself in relationships.*

I run an organization called Love Thy Neighborhood. Among other things, we recruit young adults from all over the world to relocate to our city to live together in impoverished neighborhoods and serve with understaffed urban ministries. We're like the Peace Corps but with Bibles. In my nearly two decades of working with young adults doing missions and discipleship, there's one story I've heard over and over again. It goes something like this.

A young adult named James comes to give a year of his life to serving the marginalized and being an urban missionary. And those really are the two things on his mind—service and evangelism. To James, these are the most important things about his time with LTN.

But then James starts to experience something else. In his first week, he is asked to share his entire life story—from birth to present—with his new household. As the weeks go by, he has dinner with his fellow missionaries at least twice a week. Once a week, they get together and spend a couple of hours updating one another on how their lives are going—their highs, their burdens, their worries—and pray for one another. They serve together, worship together, and do life together. James finds himself spending just as much, if not more, time with his fellow missionaries as he does engaging in missions or discipleship.

And at the end of his year of service, James is noticeably different. He is more vibrant than when he first came. He's more patient, more vulnerable, and more attuned to the people around him. He actually takes time to listen to people instead of just thinking about what he's going to say next in the conversation. Instead of seeing neighbors merely as projects, he now sees them as friends and people who have their own stories and dreams. And the day before James leaves to go back home, he comes up to me and says, "I figured out why I'm so different than when I first came. I never realized how lonely I was before. I never realized how important community is to living a full Christian life."

The thing that impacted James the most wasn't the books he read or the projects he completed. What changed his life was *community*—loving and being loved. Through LTN, I've seen over and over again that without community we are anemic versions of ourselves. We need people around us in order to thrive.

Somehow we've become accustomed to loneliness. This isn't what we were made for.

• • ● ● ● ● • • •

The book of Genesis says, "So God created mankind in his own image, in the image of God he created them; male and female he created them" (1:27).

What does this mean?

This is where the notion of *imago Dei* comes from. Every human being is made in *the image of God*. Sort of like you have mannerisms, expressions, or physical features that resemble your mom or dad, being made in the image of God means you intrinsically bear a resemblance to him in your essence. You might have your mom's eyes

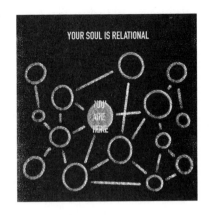

but you have God's image. This is what the Scriptures call the soul. This image is immaterial, eternal, and extremely valuable.

This essence brings with it a built-in design feature: you are *relational*. Let's think about the Trinity for a moment: God is three distinct persons as Father, Son, and Spirit—eternally loving each

other. This is how we can say that "God is love" (1 John 4:8). "God can only *be* love if God exists as a community."[1] Love requires relationships. So God is relational. Being made in the likeness of God means your soul exists for the purpose of being in a loving relationship with God and other people.

God designed your *relational* soul to express itself through your personality.[2] As we discussed in the introduction, personality can be described as "the way we perceive, process, and present." In other words, you see the world in a way that is unique to you, process your experiences through your own methods, and then present to the world with a particular style.

PERSONALITY

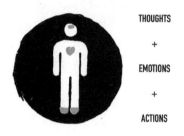

THOUGHTS

+

EMOTIONS

+

ACTIONS

As you present your personality to the world, you will do so in three ways: through your emotions, your thoughts, and your actions. It's what you feel, what you think, and what you do.

When God designed us, he intended for our personality to be well-rounded. Imagine your personality to be like spokes on a tire. God planned for it to look like a perfectly round wheel. However, each of us knows this is no longer the case. Instead, it looks like a car ran over your bike. While some spokes are in

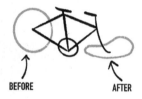

YOUR SOUL

BEFORE   AFTER

excellent condition, others are broken and deformed and could put someone's eye out. Even if you can still ride the bike, the experience is going to be bumpy at best. How did this deformation happen?

Fear, Guilt, and Shame

God wanted a deep relationship with us. Because the foundation of any healthy relationship is trust, God wanted us to trust him. He wanted us to trust his intentions, his methods, and his timing. He wanted us to trust that he was with us and for us. Instead of trusting God, we became mistrusting. We backed over the wheel of our soul.

Every healthy relationship is built on the foundation of trust. Without trust, the relationship begins to fracture. In the Garden of Eden, we committed the original sin—mistrust. We mistrusted God and began to take matters into our own hands. Humanity fell, and paradise slipped from our grip. Adam and Eve manifested the first expressions of our underlying emotions of fear, guilt, and shame. Fear tells us we are in constant danger of losing something precious. Guilt tells us we are culpable for the sinful actions or inactions we've committed. Shame tells us we are defective, and our exposure will humiliate us. This pain is too great to bear, so we devise tactics to survive and manipulate. We see all of this on display in Adam and Eve.

In their fear, they hide (Genesis 3:8).

In their guilt, they blame (Genesis 3:12–13).

In their shame, they cover themselves (Genesis 3:7).

These same emotions are still active in our lives today. They have affected our family of origin, our life choices, and our experiences. Our culture, our DNA, our gender, our ethnicity—*all* of life has been distorted by these three underlying emotions.

Like Adam and Eve, we devise tactics to survive these emotions and manipulate our experiences. We try to find solutions to our problems that don't require us to trust God. These underlying emotions produce a  unique deadly sin for each personality within the Enneagram. We will see that for each type, the deadly sin does not feel like sin. Instead, it likely feels comforting, familiar, and reasonable. It's like we are drinking bleach because we have grown to prefer the taste over fresh water. And we can't see that it's killing us.

We are guilty because of the sins we commit. We are wounded because of the sins committed against us. And sadly, we commit our greatest sins out of our deepest wounds.

We are no longer the way we were intended to be. While our

souls still contain the essence of the *imago Dei*, these distortions are now present within us and make themselves known in our personalities. Because of this, a civil war is waging inside our soul.

Your True Self and False Self

We have a part of ourselves that remembers and reflects our True Self in Christ and another part of us that is our False Self—determined to have its independence from God. Some people (using the apostle Paul's words) refer to this as the Spirit and the flesh (Romans 7:4–6). Whatever you call it, this warfare between these two selves is raging within us 24-7.

Your True Self is the part of you that desires healthy relational connection with others. When this True Self manifests in your personality, it is the clearest glimpse of the *imago Dei* in you—reflecting the character, traits, and presence of God to the world. This is who you are "in Christ" and who God intended you to be.

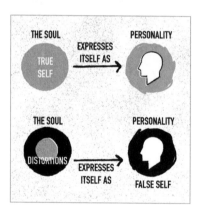

However, as the distortions of your soul manifest in your personality, a False Self emerges. This part of us is convinced that compromises are necessary for survival. This False Self tells us that our needs won't be met unless we let *it* take care of us. It tells us that God has abandoned us and that we don't need him anyway. The False Self is both wounded and one that wounds. It's your attempt to utilize sin to cope with sin. It's like getting drunk today to cope with your guilt from getting drunk yesterday. It's an adapted self that mistrusts God—a persona that rationalizes and excuses sin. It is a prison you lock yourself in.[3]

With both our True Self and our False Self at play in our lives, we live as an Expressed Self.[4] Our Expressed Self is both True and False, both resourceful and unresourceful, both free and enslaved. Our reality is not either-or but both-and. Your Personality and your Expressed Self are one and the same—full of goodness and evil, truth and distortions, strengths and scars.

Both our True Self and our False Self make themselves known in our relationships.

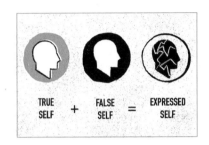

The quality of your life is determined by the quality of your relationships. This is why Jesus prayed for his followers, "I pray also for those who will believe in me . . . that all of them may be one, Father, just as you are in me and I am in you. May they also be in us so that the world may believe that you have sent me" (John 17:20–21). Jesus prayed that we would be capable of intimacy and community.

How will the world know we are Christians? By our approach to relationships.[5]

When you show up for your relationships, what is your relational style? This is where the Enneagram can help.

CHAPTER 2

THE
ENNEAGRAM

*Everyone approaches
relationships in their own way.
What's your style?*

There are stories from the Great Plains of farmers going out in the winter to care for their animals during a blizzard, only to get lost in the blinding snow on their way back to the house. They'd stumble their way forward, certain that their home was just a bit further ahead. Instead, each blind step would lead them farther away from shelter and safety. Their bodies would be discovered months later when spring arrived and the snow melted.

To keep themselves from a wandering death, farmers in the Great Plains began to tie a rope around their waist when they went outside. One end of the rope served as a belt, while the other end was tied to a post by their home. Whether it was a blizzard in the summer or a tornado in the spring, the farmer simply had to follow the rope to get back home. Though they were blind and disoriented, trusting the rope saved their lives.

The rope couldn't breathe life into the lungs of the farmer or tell them why they were a farmer, but it could definitely keep them from getting lost and point them in the right direction in the middle of a blizzard. The Enneagram is a rope that can help bring you back home.

· · ● ● ● ● · · ·

To uncover our relational style, we'll first need to explore the basics of the Enneagram.

What makes the Enneagram so useful? The Enneagram factors in both the spiritual and psychological complexity of people. It begins with the premise that no two people are the same. We are an unwieldy mixture of life experiences, motivations, longings, and interpersonal styles. We are the result of nature and nurture, of mystery and facts. A few years ago, one woman told me, "I used to avoid the Enneagram because I thought its goal was to put me in a box. In reality, the Enneagram helped me see how I put *myself* in the box." The Enneagram gives us clues into the deeper terrain within our soul, where God is working to confront, affirm, and heal us.

The Enneagram is a powerful diagnostic tool. Developed over thousands of years through a variety of people, it has become a highly useful guardian against self-deception. The Enneagram works like a mirror that reflects both our truthfulness and falsehood back to us. Its recent surge in popularity is due in large part to how easy it is to use while providing such robust insights.

Like the Location Services on our phones that show us our bearings, the Enneagram has the ability to help us understand where we are in our relationships with other people and ourselves.

It shows us the way other people experience us. The Enneagram helps us see many of the beliefs that fuel our actions and inactions, some we might not even be aware of. The self-awareness gained through the Enneagram gives us language to talk about our desires and our sins. In many ways, the Enneagram is also more about what we *don't* see than what we do. It shows us our fixations as well as our blind spots.

Likewise, the Enneagram increases our empathy for the personality and pain of others. How many times have we assumed people are doing things intentionally to hurt us when in reality it was a difference in the way we perceive, process, and present? As Atticus Finch says in *To Kill a Mockingbird*, "You never really understand a person until you consider things from his point of view . . . until you climb into his skin and walk around in it."[1]

The Enneagram creates a road map to greater relational intimacy. So how does it work?

The Triads

As we said previously, the soul expresses itself through personality. Though we are tempted to think of ourselves in simplistic terms ("I'm not emotional," or, "I just go with my gut"), that is untrue. Personality is composed of three ingredients: our actions, emotions, and thoughts. The Bible largely refers to these three ingredients as "the heart." The biblical authors saw our actions, emotions, and thoughts as so intertwined—so inseparable—that they often referred to them through the singular term "the heart"—an ancient way of referring to personality.[2]

Enneagram teachers use slightly different language. Instead of saying "the heart" as shorthand for our actions, emotions, and thoughts, they refer to these three ingredients as the triadic centers of intelligence (or "triads" for short). The Enneagram names these

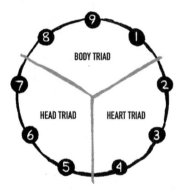

triads the Body Triad (actions), the Heart Triad (emotions), and the Head Triad (thoughts). Just as the Bible says we interpret and respond to the world through "the heart," the Enneagram draws the same conclusion using different words. Elements from each of these triads combine to compose our personality.

There are a total of nine types within the Enneagram (more on that in a moment). Three of the types fall within the Body Triad, three within the Heart Triad, and three within the Head Triad. Each of us resides primarily within one of these triads. The triad in which a type is located reveals which aspect of our personality we rely on the most. In other words, there are people who prefer to interpret the world through their bodily instincts, others through their emotions, and still others through their minds. Each of us overemphasizes one of these aspects (thinking, doing or feeling) and underutilizes the other two in the process.

Additionally, though we all are impacted by fear, guilt, and shame, our triad tends to put special emphasis on one of these emotions in particular. So the Enneagram not only reveals whether you rely on your instincts, emotions, or thinking first, but it also shows you which negative emotion you are likely to wrestle with the most. The severity of these emotions comes from what we believe we have lost—either our freedom, our identity, or our security. In turn, what has been lost leads each triad to be haunted by an existential question: *Who am I?*, *Where am I?*, or *How am I doing?*[3] When left unhealed or unacknowledged, these underlying emotions and feelings of loss fuel our False Self. Does this all seem a bit confusing? Well, let's talk through each of the triads and see if we can clear things up.

The Body Triad

The Body Triad includes types Eight, Nine, and One. They process the world primarily through their gut instincts. As a result, their body language often communicates their true feelings before their brains can recognize what they feel. They present as being grounded in the moment and focused on overcoming the threats of life by pushing through to achieve their goals. They tend to hold their ground rather than adapt. They are wrestling with the question, *How am I doing?* They have an overwhelming sense that they are not doing enough or that they are doing the wrong things. Because they are highly aware of their actions and inactions, their primary underlying emotion is *guilt*.

People who reside in this triad tend to convert many of their negative emotions into anger. Some people in this triad often feel their anger more readily than their guilt. Under this anger is often profound grief. They are likely to perceive the world as coming against them and threatening their autonomy. When they're resourceful, this triad pursues healthy independence. When they're unresourceful, they resist being held accountable and blame their problems on others.

The Heart Triad

The Heart Triad includes types Two, Three, and Four. People in this triad perceive the world as a series of interpersonal relationships. They process their experiences through their emotions. These emotions can sometimes become big and overwhelming for them. They present themselves as highly relational. They value what others

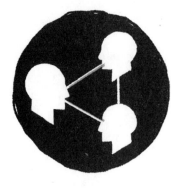

want from them and often adapt to meet those needs.

People in the Heart Triad are often grappling with the question, *Who am I?* Because this is a question about identity (and the belief that theirs is deformed or lacking), their primary underlying emotion is *shame*. At various levels, they are embarrassed about who they are, feel defective, and worry about being rejected by others. When they're resourceful, people in the Heart Triad seek out healthy connections with others and themselves. When they're unresourceful, they create personas.

The Head Triad

The Head Triad includes types Five, Six, and Seven. People in this triad tend to perceive the world as a series of complex obstacles to be navigated. They process the world primarily through their minds. As a result, they can often become out of touch with both their bodies and their emotions. They present themselves as observant, organized, and dependable.

People in the Head Triad are haunted by the question, *Where am I?* They tend to be preoccupied about their relationships to infor-

mation, safety, and pleasure. Their underlying emotion is *fear*. They are anxious and scared about the obstacles of life harming them. To ease their fears and make them feel safe, people in this triad are always on the hunt for more resources and support. When they're resourceful, they seek out and trust healthy support systems. When they're unresourceful, they become obsessive and stifled by anxiety.

Now that you understand the triads and which underlying emotion each gravitates toward, let's look at the individual types.

The Nine Enneagram Types

The Enneagram breaks human personality down into nine types. Each of these types contains distinct personality characteristics. Every person contains elements of all nine types to greater or lesser degrees. However, we identify most readily with a single type. Whichever type we identify with the most is our *core type*.

All nine of the types have both True Self (resourceful) traits and False Self (unresourceful) traits. In addition, each type has a primary strategy—a way of pursuing the identity, security, or freedom they are seeking. We will explore each type in depth in separate chapters. Let's take a look at an overview of the traits of all nine types.

Type One: The Reformer

Resourceful: Honest, hardworking, devoted to practical action, highly ethical, orderly, appropriate, conscientious
Unresourceful: Judgmental, rigid, harsh, inflexible, demanding, conditional, micromanaging, critical, controlling
Primary Strategy: Doing the right thing
Triad: Body

Type Two: The Helper

Resourceful: Generous, supportive, encouraging, thoughtful, caregiving, compassionate, sacrificial
Unresourceful: Intrusive, possessive, codependent, people-pleasing, needs to be needed, angry
Primary Strategy: Helping others
Triad: Heart

Type Three: The Achiever

Resourceful: Efficient, goal-oriented, communicator, driven, motivating, adaptable, successful, competent
Unresourceful: Image-conscious, superficial, addicted to positive attention, shallow, inauthentic, manipulative
Primary Strategy: Succeeding
Triad: Heart

Type Four: The Originalist

Resourceful: Creative, expressive, deep, authentic, intense, heightened sense of beauty, emotionally intuitive
Unresourceful: Overreactive, temperamental, dramatic, snobbish, dissatisfied, feels misunderstood
Primary Strategy: Being unique
Triad: Heart

Type Five: The Investigator

Resourceful: Thinker, wise, objective, scholarly, perceptive, insightful, intelligent, witty, reflective
Unresourceful: Relationally detached, nonresponsive, isolated, reclusive, hoarding, uncaring
Primary Strategy: Figuring it out
Triad: Head

Type Six: The Loyalist

Resourceful: Faithful, committed, responsible, prepared, dependable, systematic, honorable, committed to security
Unresourceful: Skeptical, catastrophic thinker, anxious, self-doubter, uptight, rigid, wary, reluctant
Primary Strategy: Loyalty
Triad: Head

Type Seven: The Enthusiast

Resourceful: Excited, joyful, childlike wonder, playful, excitable, optimistic, curious, imaginative, funny

Unresourceful: Scattered, unreliable, escapist, pain-avoidant, uncommitted, irresponsible, juvenile, addicted, narcissistic, demanding

Primary Strategy: Enjoying life

Triad: Head

Type Eight: The Protector

Resourceful: Strong, leader, commanding, prophetic, assertive, self-confident, intense, high energy, empathetic, confident

Unresourceful: Aggressive, domineering, hostile, insensitive, controlling, vengeful, won't listen, always feels threatened

Primary Strategy: Staying in control

Triad: Body

Type Nine: The Peacemaker

Resourceful: Easygoing, calm, kind, accepting, thoughtful, reassuring, receptive, flexible, patient, reconciler

Unresourceful: Passive, stubborn, resigned, passive-aggressive, avoids conflict, procrastinating, indecisive

Primary Strategy: Cultivating harmony

Triad: Body

Three more important thoughts regarding the types: First, while there is a great deal of debate about the age at which our type forms, almost all teachers agree it is formed by early adulthood at the latest. The degree to which either we are born as our type or our environment forms our type remains a mystery. Two children can experience the same events and be different types, so we cannot attribute our personality to our childhood alone. All we can say is that both nature (our DNA) and nurture (our life experiences) play a significant role, and that by the time we reach young adulthood, we have solidified into our core type.

Second, our core type never changes. Some people may identify as a different type in the future, but that is not because their core type changed. Rather, they gained more self-clarity about their core motivations and way of relating. They are simply going from "mis-typed" to their correct core type.

Third, a quick note about the order of the types in this book. You will notice that the next chapter begins with type Eight as opposed to type One. This is because I have arranged the content by triad. We will begin in the Body Triad (Eight, Nine, One) before moving on to the Heart Triad (Two, Three, Four) and concluding with the Head Triad (Five, Six, Seven).

With these things in mind, it's time to discover the way you relate.

HOW TO DISCOVER YOUR TYPE

When it comes to figuring out your type, here are a few tips to help you as you explore each chapter:

1. Focus on the motivations, not the behaviors. All types behave in universal ways at one time or another. It's not about what you do but why you do it.
2. Remember yourself in early adulthood. This is the most acute version of you and is likely a good indicator of your type.
3. Search for who you are, not who you'd prefer to be. The goal is to find a mirror for self-clarity, not become an actor taking on a new role.

4. Pay attention to your embarrassment. If you're reading about a type and begin to feel self-conscious, it may be a sign that you're reading about yourself.
5. Don't expect to identify with every aspect of the description. No two people are alike. You may identify with most of the type but likely not all of it.
6. Self-clarity is a process. The first stage is embarrassment over our flaws. The second stage allows us to see our gifts. The third stage lets us accept both.
7. Write One to Nine on a piece of paper and scratch off the ones you know aren't you. This will help you narrow down the options as you decide your core type.
8. Talk with friends and family and let them give you feedback. Ask trusted people how they experience you and what they see motivating you.

11 RULES FOR THE ENNEAGRAM

As you discover your core type and begin to explore the Enneagram, here are a few guardrails to get the most out of this tool and avoid misusing it:

1. Don't sound like a crazy cult member. Don't talk in numbers all the time. It's weird. It freaks people out. It makes others feel stupid and like outsiders.
2. Don't weaponize the Enneagram. Don't use the Enneagram as an excuse for your bad behavior. Don't use it to manipulate others or put them in a box.
3. Don't type other people. You don't know their motives. This isn't a party trick. We're dealing with people's souls and stories. Handle with care.

4. Don't oversimplify it. People are complex. This is a complex tool. Everyone is different. Don't undo the Enneagram's benefits by turning people into caricatures.

5. It's not God and it's not Scripture. It is a tool for self-clarity. Self-clarity is for communion with God. God transforms us, not the Enneagram.

6. It's not perfect. All tools are flawed, but some are useful. Have realistic expectations for the Enneagram and how it can help you.

7. Be honest with yourself. This can only be helpful if you avoid deceit. Disowning your gifts isn't humility. It's self-deception.

8. You have all nine types inside you. You aren't just your core type. Notice which types you utilize and which ones you have disowned.

9. Find a community to journey with you. Our self-evaluation can either be too positive or too negative. Friends give us clarity and encouragement.

10. Let God hold your story and your complexity. You won't discover anything here that God doesn't already know. Let him lovingly hold your discoveries.

11. It will get worse before it gets better. Self-awareness may leave you feeling exposed, ashamed, and resistant. Abundant life is lived in reality.

THE BODY TRIAD
Searching for Freedom

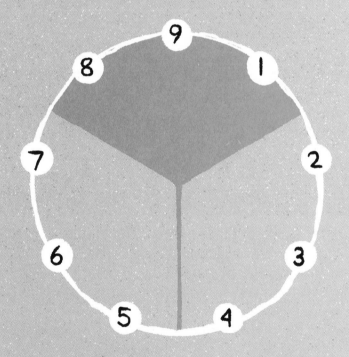

CHAPTER 3

TYPE EIGHT
THE PROTECTOR

Your protection comes from God, not your power.

There is a story in my circle about a woman I know. The story goes that one night she and her husband were at home watching the C-SPAN coverage of a town hall meeting. Citizens were stepping up to the microphone and sharing their impassioned opinions on some issue like hotel taxes or public school field trip incentives. It's unclear what the topic was, but I know this much: the council members were set to vote in less than an hour and they had clearly made up their minds already. The vote was not going to go in the direction my friends thought best.

As they sat at home watching, the woman stopped yelling at the TV when she suddenly stood up and announced she needed to step outside to get some fresh air. As her husband continued to watch the coverage, he became confused as ten minutes and then twenty minutes passed without his wife returning. Suddenly, on live TV, the chamber doors flew open as the husband watched a familiar face enter the room. In walked his wife. As citizens parted her path like Moses through the Red Sea, she made her way toward the microphone. With a cool, Southern drawl, she introduced herself to the men behind the podium. The next several minutes consisted of a suave, charismatic, fiery speech that was equal parts chastising and visionary. She existed somewhere between a fire-and-brimstone preacher and William Wallace. No one dared to interrupt her. She said her piece, stared the men in the eyes, turned around and left.

By the time she arrived back to her husband, the council members had voted in favor of her position. She also picked up some ice cream on the way home.

If you can see yourself taking charge as this woman did, you may be an Eight.

True Self

At their best, the Eight is strong and intense. Self-confident, assertive, and decisive, they often make a natural leader. Their language

is often either opposing or commanding. One Eight I know starts many of her sentences with, "You know what you should do? I'll tell you." Eights are often fiercely independent thinkers, which means rules and opinions have less influence over them than people with any other type. In other words, they can be rebellious. When healthy, this can be quite useful in dismantling unjust or broken norms. Unlike others who may be prone to beat around the bush or dance around an issue, the Eight likes to have problems out in the open where they can challenge issues directly. They hate lack of clarity in conversations and want direct answers—even if those answers are bad news. With the Eight, clarity is king.

Gifted at ignoring their fears when bravery is called for, they can be bold and inspire others to confront injustice or stand up to an enemy. In fact, the Eight has a hyperawareness of the fear and anxieties of others. When they're healthy, they use their awareness of someone's fear with wisdom—either tenderly encouraging that person or protecting them from danger. A healthy Eight is capable of acknowledging and accepting their own tender feelings as well—including fear. A hallmark trait of the Eight is their desire to protect people who are suffering from injustice.

As a member of the Body Triad, the Eight often displays their power in their body language. They are typically sure-footed with a firm presence. They speak with clarity and confidence. If you've ever been with a group of Eights, there is a sense of being surrounded by concrete with a heart. They're equal parts grizzly bear and teddy bear. Of all the types, the Eight has the most energy. I'm fairly certain we could wirelessly charge our phones just by standing in the presence of an Eight. Even though they typically need less sleep, they have twice the voltage of the other types. They thrive off of intense, high-octane experiences and can easily generate this energy when needed.

The healthiest Eights share personality qualities similar to many of the prophets of the Old Testament. They carry deep convictions about right and wrong—especially related to power imbalances, injustice, or betrayal. Their nickname "The Protector" comes from their deeply held desire to use their strength to defend people who are being exploited. They empathize with people who have less than they have and often leverage their power on behalf of victims. For this reason, they often connect with God most easily through active protection of the weak and vulnerable. God's love for the poor, the outcast, and the victim holds a special place in the heart of the Eight.

False Self

When the Eight is unhealthy, they become habitually combative. They overidentify with their strength. They are a hammer that sees a world full of nails. They tend to instigate arguments and can often be demanding and uncompromising in their positions. Instead of using their strength to care for others, they use their strength to assert their dominance and control. Perceiving that the world is against them, they become aggressive and hostile. They

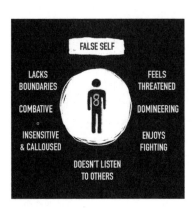

project power struggles onto the people around them, creating a situation where there are winners and losers—and they are determined that they will not be the losers. Life is a game of "King of the Mountain." Other people can try to knock them off, but we can all guess who is going to end up rolling down the hill. The Eight's relentless combat can become an exhausting experience for the people around them, who grow tired of their arguing and dominance. If someone makes them feel weak or powerless—whether intentionally or accidentally—an unhealthy Eight can become vengeful, driven by a deep desire to get even.

An unhealthy Eight rarely sees people as equals or peers. They see people in hierarchical terms. People are either strong enough that they respect them, weak enough that they must be protected, or threatening enough that they must be attacked. They smell fear like a shark smells blood. All of this makes peer-to-peer friendships very challenging.

An unhealthy Eight sees tender emotions and sensitive topics as weaknesses that hold people back from becoming stronger. As a result, they become insensitive and calloused as they fail to handle other people with appropriate care. I once witnessed an older Eight barge into a trauma therapy session and declare in a singsong voice, "Oooh! Are we talking about our feeeeliings?" followed by laughter.

When unhealthy, they refuse to listen to others and quickly dismiss ideas that do not affirm their own. In fact, the number one complaint by those in close relationships with an unhealthy Eight is, "I don't feel heard by them." When they aren't healthy, they have little regard for personal boundaries and will sometimes defy any attempts to establish them. In some cases, the Eight enjoys the energy of arguing and fighting so much that they intentionally escalate battles while ignoring the pain they may be causing other people. I was once drawn into an argument with an Eight that became far more aggressive and argumentative than necessary. Their presence was so intimidating to the other person in the room that he stopped speaking and melted into the sofa. After it was over, the Eight stood up, stretched, and said, "That was fun!"

The unhealthy Eight has a special attraction to fighting. Some Eights will trick themselves into thinking that their relentless fighting is on behalf of God. They may underscore the single time that Jesus flipped the money changers' tables in the temple while minimizing Jesus' teachings on forgiveness, peace, and gentleness. Their prayer life and public speech become focused around fighting for good against a corrupt world. Personal confession of sin and acknowledgment of their deepest hopes or fears are usually absent from both their prayers and their relationships. They relate to God as a cause worth fighting for but not as someone they know intimately.

Childhood and Adolescence: Survival and Conflict

Many Eights look back over a childhood that seems enshrouded in a theme of *survival* and *conflict*. A lot of Eights grew up in conflict-heavy environments and share that they often felt weak and attacked as kids. Some Eights came from families or communities that had a lot of aggressive contact—headlocks, wrestling, shoulder punches, teasing. Some of their fundamental relationships felt a bit like a den of bears wrestling with one another, where the lines between play and dominance get blurry. In other cases, I know several Eights who felt attacked not by people but by disease. They had major prolonged childhood illnesses that could have killed them. In either case, the child Eight felt bullied or abused by something bigger or stronger than they were. Some Eights didn't feel personally attacked but instead took on the role of protector for the sake of the more vulnerable members of their family. I know several Eights who had to protect their siblings from abusive parents or bullies at school.

THE CHILDHOOD THEME OF THE EIGHT IS SURVIVAL AND COMBAT.

In their youth, these experiences of survival and conflict led the Eight to the conclusion that *it's not okay to be vulnerable or to trust anyone*.[1] Whether being attacked by people or by disease or needing to protect others, many Eights did not feel adequately protected, and felt it was up to them to defend themselves and the people they loved. In warfare, weaknesses are liabilities, and there are few liabilities greater than trusting the wrong person. As a result, the Eight became untrusting of others. One Eight told me, "In my family, I had to deny my weaknesses because if they were discovered, they were exploited. If people saw my weaknesses, they were used against me, so I learned it wasn't safe to show them."

All of these concerns about betrayal and power struggles left the Eight *afraid of being harmed or controlled by others*.[2] I know that *afraid* is essentially a trigger word to pick a fight with an Eight (please do not punch me), but what better word could we use? Aversion? Existential dread? The-emotion-that-shall-not-be-named? When people misuse their power, people suffer. The Eight felt betrayed and dominated by others so they naturally became scared of being hurt or controlled—especially by people who had proven to be untrustworthy or weak.

They learned to cope with threats by asserting control over their environments. In order to get their needs met, they acted bigger than they were, stronger than they were, and more in control than they were. To do this, they felt forced to fortify themselves and eradicate their weaknesses. The biggest casualty in stomping out their weakness was the loss of their childhood innocence. The Eight was forced to leave behind their purity, trust, tenderness, and blissful ignorance about the harshness of life. They had to trade in their lunch box for brass knuckles. This loss of innocence in particular would go on to haunt them into adulthood.

If you take a kid and inject them with feelings of powerlessness, experiences of betrayal, and the need to be a child soldier, you end up with someone who is experiencing a lot of *anger and guilt*.[3] In fact, the Eight converts many of their emotional experiences into anger. (Anger is easier to direct and control than sadness or shame.) They're angry about the injustice of the world and what was taken from them without permission. They're mad at the unpunished guilt of others. However, hiding under their anger is often their own guilt. Though they are profoundly reluctant to acknowledge it (because admitting it to themselves or others would be a sign of weakness), the Eight feels guilty for their own bad behavior. They have not faithfully done what needs to be done and have violated their own convictions. We can't call for justice for others and then ask for immunity for ourselves.

Behind their tough and powerful exterior is just a kid with a tender heart who wants someone to tell them, "I will not betray you."[4] Despite their inclination to eradicate their own weaknesses, the Eight wants someone with whom they can safely let their innocence reemerge. They want to find a corner of the world where they can move past survival and conflict and wholeheartedly trust

THE EIGHT WANTS TO PROTECT THEMSELVES.

someone to faithfully protect the tender parts of who they are. This person will need to be both strong and trustworthy.

At their core, the Eight just wants what all of us want when facing threats: *the Eight wants to protect themselves.*[5] In a world where unfaithful people throw punches, the Eight simply wants to be able to be safe from being harmed and betrayed. They want to have independence and the freedom to make their own choices without being assaulted. When they are attacked, they want to be able to have a shield (and, if needed, a sword) to defend themselves from harm.

However, somewhere deep in their personality, this emphasis on protecting themselves gets supercharged and twisted and grows into something they likely never intended.

Nurturing Your False Self: Mistaking Control for Protection

There's an old saying that goes like this: "The best defense is a good offense." The Eight applies this rule to their relationships. Instead

WHAT IS THE EIGHT WILLING TO SACRIFICE?

CLOSENESS WITH PEOPLE

GIVING & RECEIVING FORGIVENESS

HAVING & SHARING FRAGILE FEELINGS

THE IDOL OF THE PROTECTOR
CONTROL & POWER

of turning to God and trusting him, the Eight develops an alternate solution that doesn't require trust. Because they don't feel they can fully protect themselves adequately, *they settle for the false idol of control and power.*[6] For many Eights, they can't tell the difference between self-protection and control. After all, who is more protected than the person in charge? They can direct outcomes and protect their interests. No one can tell them what to do. They ask themselves the question, *How am I doing?* and now they have an answer: *As long as I'm in charge, all will be well.*

However, the idol of control and power requires sacrifices. The Eight must sacrifice closeness with people, having feelings that are fragile, and the presence of forgiveness in their life. Power and control may help us feel safe, but it can never give us what we really need. As author Philip Yancey says, "Power can do everything but the most important thing: it cannot control love."[7]

What happens when the Eight puts their trust in power and control? They grow the deadly sin of *boundlessness.*[8] Simply put, they live without boundaries. This has to do with a passion for intensity and an entitlement to be excessive. Instead of tempering their desires, they express them without restraint. In their quest for physical and sensual fulfillment, they give themselves over to whatever impulses, cravings, or hunger they have. They assert their dominance over whatever their flesh wants and dare the world to try to stop them. They push other people beyond their

HOW DOES THE EIGHT NURTURE THEIR DEADLY SIN?

limits, disregard their boundaries, and throw them off the bus when they can't keep up. In other words, they become their hunger.

Should this boundlessness attach itself to a perceived injustice, watch out! The hunger of an unhealthy Eight becomes like Godzilla attacking a city. It won't be satisfied until the whole city has been leveled and at least a few people have died. The thrill of having an enemy to fight can be intoxicating for the Eight. It's a justifiable place to openly direct all of their anger. They don't tend to lose control so much as bite down and refuse to let go. As the classic Puritan author William Gurnall wrote, "Therefore tremble, O man, at any power thou hast, except thou usest it for God. Art thou strong in body? Who hath thy strength? God, or thy lusts?"[9] Does our strength serve our sin or our God?

To cope with their fear of being harmed and controlled by others and to protect their idol of power and control, the Eight defends themselves through *denial*[10]—a psychological defense mechanism by which the Eight unconsciously negates something that makes them feel anxious by disavowing its very existence. They utilize denial, especially regarding their own perceived vulnerabilities or weaknesses. Unlike deceit, which involves an awareness of the truth, denial prohibits the ability to see the truth. Denial often involves minimizing the severity of a problem. This leaves the Eight unaware of the true status of their relationships or problems in life.

I once sat and listened to a spouse describe to their Eight wife various frustrations he was having in their marriage—most of which had to do with her dominating and controlling tendencies. I then asked the Eight to repeat back to me what she heard her spouse say. She was incapable of restating her husband's remarks with any accuracy. Her denial had edited out the things she didn't want to hear until all she was left with was a fabricated memory. She protected her ego at the expense of reality.

We need to keep in mind the hardship that the Eight has experienced. Many Eights felt powerless as children and betrayed by people they trusted. Their desire for control grew from the wound of power being used against them. One Eight shared, "I didn't have any social capital as a kid. Both in my family and in my social group, I was bullied, exploited, and powerless. Finally, when I was a teen, I slowly woke up to my strength and could finally defend myself." Another shared, "I don't remember any moment of my childhood when I fully relied on any adult. I loved them, but I was never fully vulnerable or trusted them to deeply care for me. I couldn't rely on them. And honestly, I still feel that way." That is a heavy burden for a child to bear. Just because they *could* bear it doesn't mean they *should*.

What makes the deadly sins for each type so seductive is that in the context of our stories, they feel justifiable. They don't feel evil. They feel warranted. Mistaking boundlessness as a necessary evil in life, the Eight reframes their sin into something necessary. *The Eight believes the injustice and weakness of others justifies their boundlessness.* Their lack of boundaries and their willful dominance are rationalized by blaming others for their injustices (whether real or merely perceived). Additionally, the Eight blames others for being too weak to stop them. Blame shifting, scapegoating, and gaslighting are common tactics utilized by an unhealthy Eight in their attempt to justify their own poor actions. This allows the Eight to confuse their own boundlessness with justice.

Your Encounter with Jesus, the True Protector

As the Eight encounters Jesus, they discover that he empathizes with their pain. *Like the Eight, Jesus was attacked by unjust people and stripped of his freedom.* It seemed that every chapter of Jesus' life was marked by people who abused their power against him. King Herod tried to kill him as an infant. The Pharisees tried to stone him. The teachers of the law tried to trap him. The crowds tried to force him to become their king. The Roman government failed to protect him. The Sadducees con-

ducted an unjust trial against him. One of his best friends betrayed him. When he was given a window of opportunity to be released from his crucifixion, the crowds requested that a murderer—an insurrectionist named Barabbas—be released instead of Jesus. He died at the hands of a corrupt people and a corrupt system.

If anyone ever had a good reason not to trust people, it was Jesus. If I were him, I would have burned it all down. Fool me once, shame on you. Fool me twice, legions of angels come to give you boils, diarrhea, and death. Jesus understands firsthand what it means to be betrayed and hurt by people. He knows what it's like to suffer injustice.

LIKE THE EIGHT, JESUS WAS ATTACKED
BY UNJUST PEOPLE AND STRIPPED OF HIS FREEDOM.

Jesus also displays his authority and mastery of living well. *Jesus affirms the True Self of the Eight by confronting evil and pursuing justice.* Jesus upheld redemptive conflict as valuable and necessary. In the Gospels, we see him rebuke, confront, and publicly challenge the corrupt religious leaders. In Matthew 23, we see him bring the heat when he says, "Woe to you, teachers of the law and Pharisees, you hypocrites!" (v. 27).

Jesus had little concern about public opinion when it came to speaking the truth. In the Sermon on the Mount, Jesus declares, "Blessed are those who hunger and thirst for righteousness, for they will be filled" (Matthew 5:6). Because the Greek word for "righteousness" also means "justice," we can understand this verse to be a calling to both personal righteousness and societal justice. Whether his concern was about immorality or injustice, Jesus confronted people fearlessly and full of love. As Catherine Booth, cofounder of the Salvation Army, once famously said, "If we are to better the future we must disturb the present."[11]

LIKE THE EIGHT, JESUS CONFRONTED EVIL
AND PURSUED JUSTICE.

Like the Eight, Jesus protected the

vulnerable. In John 8, as Jesus was teaching in the temple, the religious leaders brought a woman before him that they had caught committing adultery. They humiliated her, announced her sin publicly, and then asked Jesus if the Law of Moses gave them permission to stone her. Their goal was to use her to trap Jesus so that the crowds would turn away from him. As pastor and author Scott Sauls says, "This is what happens in a group of people who claim to have 'sound theology' but are lacking in love."[12]

To the surprise of the religious leaders, Jesus defended her by redirecting everyone's attention to their own sin. He told them, "Let any one of you who is without sin be the first to throw a stone at her" (John 8:7). No one met the criteria. One at a time, they all dropped their stones and left. After her accusers had departed, Jesus then told the woman, "Neither do I condemn you . . . Go now and leave your life of sin" (v. 11). The one man justified to throw stones at a sinful woman used his strength to protect her instead.

However, Jesus also confronts the False Self of the Eight by controlling his strength. The notion that the God of the universe shrank down to become an embryo is astonishing. Perhaps even more stunning are the events surrounding his arrest. When Jesus was being arrested, Peter jumped in to protect his friend by attacking a temple guard and cutting his ear off. In the first century, temple guards were like hit men for the Mafia. They weren't doing God's work. They were corrupt, and their presence only spelled bad news for everyone there.[13]

JESUS CONFRONTS THE EIGHT BY
CONTROLLING HIS STRENGTH.

If a Nazi or the Wicked Witch of the West showed up at my front door, I wouldn't have a lot of confusion about their motives. Peter's reaction is understandable. But how does Jesus respond? He tells Peter his actions are *wrong.* He reminds everyone that he has enough power to call heavenly beings down to protect him. Instead, he heals the ear of the guard and withholds the onslaught of angels at his disposal. Power tends to cause suffering; love absorbs it. Jesus controls his strength in favor of love. As my pastor Jamaal Williams says, "Meekness is not weakness; it's controlled strength."

Likewise, Jesus was merciful to both his enemies and his friends who betrayed him. Immediately following Jesus' arrest, we see Peter deny knowing him. The friend who had said he would follow Jesus to the end bailed on him when times got tough. Shortly after, as Jesus hung on the cross (still possessing the ability to hit the nuclear launch button to rain down fire on his oppressors), he *prayed* for those actively mocking and assaulting him. Luke 23:34 tells us he prayed, "Father, forgive them, for they do not know what they are doing." Later, he extends this same forgiveness to Peter! This degree of forgiveness is so radical and unnatural that Jesus may as well have reversed gravity while he was at it. It makes even the best instincts of human nature look like a puppy mill in contrast. To trust God's eternal justice, we must release our grip on our reactive justice.

How did Jesus do this? How was it possible for Jesus to display such authority and confront evil, even after being betrayed, without ever succumbing to the deadly sin of boundlessness? Why didn't he *need* to be in control? *Jesus believed the Father would never betray him.* Jesus was not naive about the hearts of people. He was not shocked by Judas's betrayal or Peter's failure. He understood the agenda of the religious leaders. He knew that the crowds often loved the benefits of his miracles more than him. And he also knew that the Father's love and faithfulness are pure and trustworthy. The book of Psalms confirms this: "I will not take my love from him, nor will I ever betray my faithfulness. I will not violate my covenant or alter what my lips have uttered" (89:33–34). By trusting God's faithfulness, Jesus could also trust that there was no need to assert control, to direct every outcome, to take revenge, or to seek vindication. Revenge is a quick fix. Mercy endures forever.

Redeeming Your True Self: From Dominance to Innocence

God knows the Eight harbors difficult memories of battles, conflict, and survival. He understands why they live with a sense that they can't be vulnerable or trust people. He knows about their fear of betrayal and their loss of innocence that has led them to worship power and boundlessness. God looks them in the eyes and draws them into his strong arms. In faithfulness, honor and purity, God says to the Eight, "I will never betray you." The Eight finds in the gospel the very thing they want—namely, the freedom to defend themselves and others from injustice and to make their own choices.

THE EIGHT IS GIVEN THE GOOD NEWS,
"I WILL NOT BETRAY YOU."

God will never betray his people. Betrayal is not part of his character. Second Timothy tells us that God's faithfulness is not based on our faithfulness: "If we are faithless, he remains faithful, for he cannot disown himself" (2:13). When Jesus talks about his followers, he says, "I give them eternal life, and they shall never perish; no one will snatch them out of my hand" (John 10:28). His character is trustworthy. He hates the murder of innocent people (Proverbs 6:17). He hates when justice is perverted by acquitting guilty people and condemning innocent people (Proverbs 17:15). He despises cheating for personal gain (Deuteronomy 25:13–16). There is no one more loyal and no greater voice against injustice than God himself.

Jesus values freedom. He gave people options and then let them choose. When the rich young ruler heard a teaching he couldn't stomach, Jesus let him walk away (Matthew 19:16–22). When Satan asked to sift Peter like wheat and test him, Jesus did not prevent it. He only told Peter that he had prayed for him (Luke 22:31–32). He knew of Judas's forthcoming betrayal and chose only to expose it but not to prevent Judas's actions (Mark 14:17–20). When crowds became disillusioned with Jesus and abandoned him, he turned and gave the same option to his disciples: "You do not want to leave too, do you?" (John 6:67). "Take up your *cross* and follow me" is, as Philip Yancey says, "the least manipulative invitation that has ever been given."[14] Simply put, Jesus respected human freedom. He wants us to choose to love him freely, not by force.

Pastor and author Dane Ortlund writes, "[Jesus] does not love like us. We love until we are betrayed. Jesus continued to the cross despite betrayal. We love until we are forsaken. Jesus loved through forsakenness. We love up to a limit. Jesus loves to the end."[15] Jesus invites the Eight to trust him by giving up their idol of control and power and turning away from their boundlessness.

What would happen if the Eight believed that God would never betray them? What if the Holy Spirit worked the power and protection of God's presence deep into their fibers? The Eight can stop feeling the need to excessively wrestle power from others through domination or rebellion when they believe their needs will be heard and cared for by God. By seeing that Jesus himself has settled the debts of sin through his sacrifice on the cross, the Eight no longer has to. Their relationship with intensity, conflict, and revenge can be healed. They come to see that no level of personal autonomy can satisfy what their soul truly wants. What their soul truly wants they have found in Jesus himself. The Eight could choose to follow Jesus as a disciple—to take on his approach to life and his way of relating.

To counteract their boundlessness, the Eight will want to practice the virtue of *innocence*.[16] Because hardships and suffering forced the Eight to give up their childhood innocence early in life, the attributes that develop from this innocence—compassion, tenderness, and vulnerability—are often underdeveloped. They're key to following Jesus and also essential for our relationships to flourish. To develop these attributes, the Eight must reconnect with their lost innocence. (This innocence should not be confused with the innocence given to us through Christ's sacrifice in response to our sin. That innocence is crucial, but we are talking about something different here.) Many Eights already possess a natural attraction to the innocence of others. We see this in their affection for babies, children, and even animals. Though they honor it in others, they often fail to honor it in themselves. Many Eights confess they want to let others deeper into their hearts but don't know how. Innocence is the pathway.

TO COUNTERACT BOUNDLESSNESS, PRACTICE INNOCENCE.

BE VULNERABLE, TENDER, AND TRUSTING WITHOUT CONTROLLING OUTCOMES.

Innocence is about reconnecting with our inner child. This may sound odd at first, but Jesus actually calls his disciples to do this very thing. In Matthew 18:3, he says, "Truly I tell you, unless you change and become like little children, you will never enter the kingdom of heaven." Innocence is teachable and trusting, forgiving and merciful. Innocence is not fiercely independent but has needs and relies on others to have those needs met. Innocence responds tenderly to the pain of others through service and empathy. Innocence gives us permission to cry, to grieve, and to sometimes feel confused. It allows us to experience the moment just as it is without the need to control it. Though the world still needs people who are brave, strong, and direct, it also needs people who are "as shrewd as snakes and as innocent as doves" (Matthew 10:16).

When the Eight practices innocence, their life begins to grow a variety of good fruit. *First, practicing innocence allows them to develop tenderness.* They learn to feel and express their hurt feelings and sensitive emotions. Holding the tenderness of others is hard, but letting others hold our own tenderness is often harder. It takes real strength to trust others with our wounds and dreams. In the words of poet Gretel Ehrlich, "To be tough is to be fragile; to be tender is to be truly fierce."[17]

Second, practicing innocence allows them to become merciful. Mercy allows the Eight to redirect their energy away from revenge toward compassion and kindness. They come to see why Jesus said, "Blessed are the merciful, for they shall receive mercy" (Matthew 5:7 ESV). As the Eight comes to recognize how merciful God has been to them for their own failures, they learn to do the same for others.

Finally, practicing innocence allows them to live interdependently. Moving beyond a hierarchical view of relationships in which the Eight is often independent and looks down on weaker people as needy, they begin to establish trusting, interdependent relationships. They learn to appropriately rely on others and respect people's boundaries. They don't require people to sacrifice their own convictions or needs but cultivate a balanced relationship in which neither person controls the other.

Discipleship: Adopting a Cause and Accountability

To keep themselves from falling back into the allure of control and boundlessness, the Eight will want to walk with Jesus through spiritual disciplines. Discipline brings freedom. Pastor and author AJ Sherrill recommends two disciplines.[18] *The first spiritual discipline is taking on a good cause.* Doing so will direct the Eight's energy and desire for justice to benefit people in need. Whether serving the homeless, protecting unborn children, combating racism, or helping refugees from war-torn countries, the boldness of the Eight can make a difference. I know one Eight who partners with former Navy Seals to infiltrate child-trafficking rings around the world. He uses his strength and empathy by helping exploited children escape some of the most horrific conditions a person can experience.

The second spiritual discipline is accountability with people they trust. The Eight tends to avoid vulnerability. They also tend to be unaware of how other people experience them. The Eight will need to seek out, commit to, and follow through on a regular time of meeting with others for the purpose of mutual vulnerability and accountability. (I recommend doing this weekly or biweekly.) It's important that the Eight does not lead the group or have authority over others in the group. Whether with a small group from church or a group of friends, the Eight should be aware that their tendency to project a strong, fearless presence makes others reluctant to share honest feedback. This is counterproductive to accountability. For this reason, the Eight will need to bear responsibility for dialing down their intensity, softening their presence, and humbly receiving any feedback that comes their way.

When we consider the process of transformation, we should not be naive. The True Self is a fighter, but so is the False Self. It is a suicide bomber. If it cannot win, it will try its best to do as much destruction during its downfall as possible. However, as the Eight walks with Jesus in both strength *and* innocence, they will be shaped more into the likeness of their teacher. Weakness shall become strength. Surrender shall become victory. The last shall become first.

The True Self of the Eight reflects God's power and protection.[19] The Eight helps the world see what the presence of God can do in our lives. As 2 Timothy 1:7 says, "For God gave us a spirit not of fear but of power and love and self-control" (ESV). The Eight reminds us that God leverages his strength for others and calls us to do the same. Psalm 82:3 says, "Defend the weak and the fatherless; uphold the cause of the poor and the oppressed." They help

THE EIGHT REFLECTS GOD'S POWER & PROTECTION.

others to see that God will drive out all our fear. Isaiah 41:10 tells us, "Do not fear, for I am with you; do not be dismayed, for I am your God. I will strengthen you and help you, I will uphold you with my righteous right hand." When the Eight follows Jesus in both justice and mercy, they help us believe that God is righting the wrongs of this world with a firm but tender hand.

Practical Tips for the Eight

1. Practice vulnerability. Find a couple close, trusted friends you can share tender feelings, anxieties, and weaknesses with.
2. Avoid pushing others as hard as you push yourself. You have far more energy than other types. Be realistic with other people's limits and abilities.
3. Remember that sparring is stimulating to you but often not to others. While you enjoy it, other people may find it intimidating or exhausting.
4. Let others take the lead. Let people do things differently than you would. Withhold your comments or judgment. Support their efforts.
5. Resist dismissing other people's experience or views. Practice being empathetic, listening actively, and repeating back to them a synopsis of what they shared.
6. Praise God for being strong where you are weak. The weight of the world isn't on your shoulders. You can rest as God directs outcomes.

CHAPTER 4

TYPE NINE
THE PEACEMAKER

———•———

Your peace comes from God, not from avoidance.

For many years, I worked at a homeless shelter. Every day, men and women would come through our doors trying to capture just a few hours of relief from the cruelty of life on the streets. We were a safe place where they could get some food, do their laundry, or store their belongings. Everybody was homeless for different reasons. I knew one guy who had to choose between paying child support or rent. He chose his kid and ended up on the streets. A lot of our guests had jobs. What they didn't have was enough income. Quite a few were still teens who had recently aged out of the foster care system with no safety net to catch them. But there were also the stereotypes—a viscous cocktail of childhood trauma, mental illness, and self-medication spelled b-e-e-r.

Every now and then, we'd look up and wave hello to Dr. Jekyll as he came through the door, only to realize that today he was Mr. Hyde, with enough liquor on his breath to disinfect a wound. It usually didn't take long for Mr. Hyde to pick a fight or yell a racial slur or put his hands on someone. Of course, it was up to the staff to address this when it happened. In my early years, I'm sad to say I usually tried to go toe-to-toe with our aggressive guests. This, of course, was utter stupidity. I can't count the number of times I was certain this would spell the end for me. When we say someone is "under the influence," it means the person normally inside the body in front of you is currently away on vacation and they've temporarily allowed a wild beast to drive the car.

However, my coworker Ben was a master at diffusing tense situations. He was the bomb squad of explosive alcoholics. Ben's affable and warm nature made him a favorite of our guests. Every day, he'd go and sit with people, asking questions about their lives. Receptive as they shared, he'd smile or grimace or laugh in response to the stories he heard. When Ben was around, people felt listened to. Then, should a guest show up under the influence or having a bad mental health day, we'd send in Ben to mediate. This usually sounded a lot like Ben listening to the person (even as many were saying fantastical, nonsensical things), using diplomatic and disarming language ("Oh, man, that sounds tough! Let's go talk about it away from everyone else") and eventually coaxing the guest out the door ("How 'bout we do this: Why don't you come back tomorrow after you've sobered up a bit and you can tell me more about it?"). Half the time, the angry guest would end up apologizing and thanking Ben before it was all over. Ben could de-escalate Congress if given the chance.

If you're receptive, easygoing, patient, and accepting like Ben, you may be a Nine.

True Self

When healthy, the Nine is peaceful, calm, and humble. They are simple and relaxed in their desires—an outward expression of their internal value of peace. These easygoing people are flexible in their agendas and patient as they tolerate delays, problems, or suffering without becoming annoyed or anxious. Both gentle and kind,

they are considerate of others and approach their lives with a soft touch. As a member of the Body Triad, the Nine's body language reflects their personality and is often loose, relaxed, and casual. In fact, the Nine has a reputation for enjoying sleep more than any of the other types, and they often

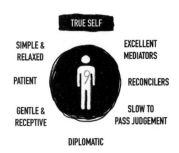

have the lowest amount of energy. Their ease and comfort are often contagious. When a Nine enters the room, people tend to breathe a little easier. Being around them is like a bubble bath for anxiety.

Nines rarely throw hand grenades into the middle of a conversation. They're thoughtful with their words—often choosing language that unites rather than divides. They're excellent listeners and often provide receptive body language and words of reassurance as people share with them. This makes those around them feel safe and supported.

Because they are gifted at being able to see multiple perspectives and points of view, the Nine is likely the most objective of all the types. Whereas some of us struggle to empathize with *anyone*, the Nine tends to be able to understand the reasons and motivations for nearly *everyone's* decisions. This allows them to be excellent mediators and diplomatic reconcilers. Because Nines are accepting and inclusive, even the lowliest outsider feels at home in their presence. Because the Nine is slow to pass judgment, people find it easy to be candidly honest and vulnerable with them. I used to tell my friend Sam that I felt like I could tell her I accidentally ran over a puppy on the way to meet her and she would still love me.

Instead of trying to appease everyone, healthy Nines declare their wants or needs (even when it means upsetting other people) and assert themselves when their boundaries are crossed. They may be easygoing, but they have a firm backbone. They're in touch with their feelings—including their anger. They work hard to intentionally engage their life and display their love for people through intentional acts of generosity and service.

Nines often feel a special connection to God when they are among nature and within the church. I think in many ways they are smitten with the same things in both. It's as though they look out at the faces in a congregation or the open bed of a forest and they just *see* the interconnected design of it all. Nines have a lot less ego than the rest of us. Many of us think our type is the one that really keeps this whole operation going. Nines know it takes all of us to make this ecosystem work.

Creation is like one of those modern photo mosaics where it's a large picture made up of little pictures. Stand close and you see a thousand detailed photos. Stand afar and you see the big picture they form together. The church is called the body of Christ. Nines know the body needs arms *and* legs, eyes *and* ears. To them, even pinky toes are vital. Everywhere they look they see an interdependent portrait of God being displayed among his people. They find pleasure and awe in being a part of this symbiotic Jesus.

False Self

When they're unhealthy, the Nine becomes allergic to conflict. Their gift of peace and desire for harmonious relationships goes septic and turns into an avoidance of conflict altogether. When conflict does arise, the unhealthy Nine becomes intangible—like a man becoming a ghost or a solid becoming a mist. They become difficult to take hold of. Your eyes can see them, but there's nothing to grab on to. They can be vague and oblivious, lacking personal conviction or engagement. The Nine indirectly resist the demands of others through an arsenal of passive-aggressive tools—appeasement, forgetfulness, procrastination, sulkiness.

The Nine develops a sort of relational narcolepsy. They struggle to stay engaged in their relationships and are prone to check out at any moment. They feel overwhelmed by life and what their relationships expect or want from them, so they withdraw and disconnect from people as well as from their own emotions. In particular, the Nine tries to disconnect from their own anger. Anger disrupts their inner peace, so, like the old myth of an ostrich with their head in the sand to avoid predators, the Nine attempts to avoid their anger in hopes that it will blow over. With their head buried to reality, the Nine can become passive, apathetic, and procrastinating—often making their situation worse.

Because of their internal vagueness, they find it hard to make decisions or find clarity. (If you've ever asked a Nine to decide where you're going for dinner, you know that immigrating to a new country is often a shorter process. It can take a while.) Often withdrawing to the background, they tend to become self-belittling and view themselves as unimportant. They struggle to identify what they want or need. They merge with the views and agendas of others and become self-forgetting. They "forget" their own priorities, their own opinions, and their own desires. Essentially, they fall asleep to their life because they fall asleep to themselves.

The unhealthy Nine is the most stubborn of all the types. Like a mule who lies down when their harness is pulled and they don't want to do something, the Nine simply stops moving. In fact, the more pressure the Nine feels, the more they resist. It's as if their mind and heart go to sleep (and their bodies soon follow). Even if they do respond to the prompts of others, their words of appeasement are generally not followed by any long-term action. The Nine has learned that if they wait long enough, people will move on and leave them alone.

The Nine can become quite lazy—especially regarding issues that matter most. They can lack initiative and follow-through and will avoid accountability. They feel guilty about both their actions and their inactions, leaving them indecisive and unsure of how to move forward. Because of their tendency to be unassertive and overly accommodating, they can become resigned to their station in life and can even behave as victims. The path they almost always prefer is the one with the least resistance.

Concerning their relationship with God, the unhealthy Nine may go through the rhythms of church life but never let those experiences rouse them. They won't wrestle with the sermon, be shaped by the liturgy, or be touched by the music. They may not even respond to the needs of the people around them. Likewise, their direct engagement with God may take a similar shape— vague, erratic prayers; dabbling in spiritual disciplines without follow-through; ignoring God's commands to take action. When unhealthy, their goal is to protect their inner peace from being disturbed. The peace of God may appeal to the unhealthy Nine, but the person of God merely seems suffocating and disruptive.

Childhood and Adolescence: Unheard and Overpowered

While many people felt dismissed as children, for the Nine the theme of being *unheard and overpowered* threads throughout their youth. The Nine was surrounded by troubles on both sides. On one side, they had the issue of family members with dominating personalities—strong opinions, swift reactions, bossiness. They could tear through their home like a tornado through a trailer park. On the other side, they had the issue of family members with passive personalities—absent, inactive, unresponsive. They were nonchalant about everything. The tornado could rip the roof off and they'd just keep watching TV.

Don Richard Riso and Russ Hudson write, "Many Nines report that they had a happy childhood,

THE CHILDHOOD THEME OF THE NINE IS BEING UNHEARD AND OVERPOWERED.

but this is not always the case. When their childhoods were more troubled, young Nines learned to cope by dissociating from the threatening and traumatic events around them and by adopting the role of Peacemaker or Mediator during family conflicts."[1] Being low-maintenance was the best way to calm down an overpowering family member. They stopped asserting themselves and began to avoid the conflict altogether. This was often accomplished by being vague and undemanding. However, their external vagueness eventually seeped inside. Many Nines never learned to actualize themselves independently—to be their own person with their own desires and ambitions. Because they merged with the agendas of others throughout their lives, many Nines can be late bloomers.

Getting caught in conflict with both their domineering and passive family members usually didn't change any outcomes or help them get their needs met. Having enough of these experiences eventually taught the Nine that *it's not okay to assert yourself.*[2] Why assert yourself if you can't change the outcome? It's like trying to direct a raging river. Asserting themselves felt either pointless or dangerous. Any attempt at being direct, self-assured, and declarative were usually ignored or overpowered. This reinforced the notion that they should be quiet, accepting and never become too confident in their positions. Their place was in the background. The problem is that you can't really build confidence if you're always on the sidelines. This left the Nine feeling overwhelmed and ill-equipped to meet the demands of their life.

Wrestling with whether or not they should ever speak up left the Nine *afraid of losing connection with others.*[3] The Nine worries that if they assert themselves, others may not like what they say. The Nine is scared that if they're too needy or cause too much tension, they'll push people away. Make too many demands, and they could find themselves being shut out, uninvited, dismissed, or discarded. They're worried that if they stir up conflict, someone might get fed up and tell them, "You've really become more trouble than you're worth." They fear rejection and abandonment. By pleasing others, they keep their world at peace.

If you take a kid and make them feel powerless and unheard and teach them to belittle their own opinions and desires, you end up with someone who is experiencing a lot of *anger and guilt.*[4] The Nine is angry that they've been overlooked and dismissed and that they feel overwhelmed by life's demands. Most Nines ignore or avoid their own anger. It just feels too threatening and overwhelming to acknowledge or wield. When their anger is left unaddressed, it stirs up inside like shaking a bottle of soda. This is why many Nines emotionally explode from time to time. However, under their anger is often guilt. Many Nines feel guilty that by taking the path of least resistance so often, their actions and inactions have violated their convictions. They have not done what needed to be done to live a robust life.

Behind their humble and gentle exterior is just a kid with a hopeful heart who wants someone to tell them, *"Your presence matters."*[5] Even though they often belittle themselves and their own importance, the Nine wants to find someone with whom their desires, opinions, wants, and needs are heard and valued. Someone who gives specific words of affirmation. They want to find someone who won't overpower them or dismiss them but instead will give them the time they need to discover who they are without growing impatient.

This is why the Nine spends so much time valuing the presence of others. They excel at making people feel seen and heard. They'll listen to long explanations or rambling stories as if there is no other place they'd rather be. They are fully present and make others feel that their presence matters. The Nine gives to others what they long to receive.

THE NINE WANTS TO BE AT PEACE.

What drives the Nine as a person? At their center, the Nine *wants to be at peace.*[6] They don't just want world peace and an end to conflict, violence, and pain; they want inner peace—to be calm and tranquil internally no matter the stresses that arise. Their hope is that if they can achieve a settled stability internally, their emotions will be safe from disturbances.

Unfortunately, buried deep somewhere in their personality, this emphasis on being at peace adapts into something else. They settle for a synthetic version of peace that poisons them instead.

Nurturing Your False Self: Mistaking Comfort for Peace

Comedian Mike Birbiglia tells a story about realizing he might have a medical problem. The issue was significant: he couldn't sleep. For months, he was barely getting a few hours of rest a night. Even when he did, he realized he had started sleepwalking. Things were getting dangerous. In trying to decide what to do, he says, "I remember thinking, *Maybe I should see a doctor.* And then I thought, *Maybe I'll eat dinner.* And I went with dinner. For years."[7] This also summarizes the Nine's new tactic for dealing with unwanted conflict.

Instead of turning to God for support to overcome obstacles, the Nine simply turns away from obstacles. Believing they can never truly be at peace, *the Nine settles for the false idol of comfort.* They seek out physical ease, freedom from pain, and avoidance of interruptions. They avoid anything that may trouble the waters of their inner calm. For the Nine, this often ends up looking like merging with others. By "going along to get along," the Nine melds with the agendas, opinions, and desires of those around them. They default to the wishes of others as an attempt to take the valleys and peaks of relationships and flatten them into a long, predictable, safe path with as little disturbance as possible. They idealize other people and minimize themselves. By focusing their attention on what others want from them, they can remain comfortably protected from any conflict that may threaten their relationships.

However, this idol of comfort requires sacrifices. They must sacrifice their own desires (in lieu of someone else's), the belief that they can make a difference, and the growth that comes from conflict. When Proverbs 27:17 says that "iron sharpens iron," it is painting a picture of healthy conflict. By avoiding conflict, the Nine ends up avoiding growth.

What happens when a Nine puts their hope in comfort? They grow the deadly sin of *sloth*. Sloth is a reluctance to exert energy and put in effort. *Sloth* can be a misleading word, since many Nines can be quite hardworking. Perhaps a better word for this deadly sin would be *indolence*—the avoidance of exertion on things that matter. Or as Enneagram teacher and former priest Clarence Thomson puts it, "They are lazy about what is most important in their lives."[8]

My son used to sleepwalk. He'd stumble into our bedroom, eyes open, and carry on nonsensical conversations with us. He'd fall in and out of responsiveness before disappearing back into his room. He was there but not there. He'd wake up the next day with no memory of what happened. This is what the Nine is like when their deadly sin is in play—present but absent. Many Nines seek outside stimulants because they have a hard time motivating themselves intrinsically. Running late, waiting for someone to prod them, and even using illegal substances can all be the means by which a Nine rouses themselves into action.

The Nine grows and nurtures this deadly sin by avoiding conflict, pursuing paths of least resistance, excessively engaging in escapist hobbies, and taking jobs that are beneath their skill set. In other cases, the Nine may be a hard worker (possibly even a workaholic) but may use work to avoid intimate relationships that feel too overwhelming. This sloth grows an ever-deepening sense of moral guilt inside due to their actions as well as their inactions. The Nine will posture themselves as "just being cautious" as a way to avoid decision making. In reality, they are simply unwilling to take actions they don't feel like doing. As one Nine said to me, "I want to do what I want to do when I want to do it . . . if I feel like doing it."

To cope with their fear of losing connection with others and to protect their idol of comfort, the Nine defends themselves through *numbing*[9]—a psychological defense mechanism that avoids conflict by numbing feelings, preferences, or convictions. Nines narcotize and distract themselves by engaging in prolonged rhythmic activities that are familiar, require very little attention, and provide comfort. The Nine develops strong routines and rituals to avoid having to be overly present and awake to their life. In addition, they become agitated or disoriented when these repetitive activities become disrupted.

We should remember that the Nine routinely felt engulfed, overwhelmed, and powerless as a child. Maybe Mom was distracted by serving everyone else and failed to tune in to her quieter child. Maybe Dad was a bit reclusive with body language that made it clear he preferred to be left alone. Maybe the house was full of children—some of whom had mastered the art of getting what they wanted. With so many agendas surrounding them, the Nine just felt a bit lost at sea. Merging with others didn't feel like a mistake; it felt like a life raft. But other people can't live our lives for us. Instead of developing the internal muscles to declare our identity, we let others decide who we are. It's wrong to expect other people to make our choices for us. We tell ourselves it's because they're more capable, but belittlement is not humility. At some point, it's just an excuse to go back to bed.

Each of the types has an affection for their deadly sin. It doesn't feel evil or destructive so much as it feels natural and familiar. *The Nine believes the overwhelming demands of others justify their sloth.* The blaming tone in this statement also reveals the repressed anger of the Nine. Often, the Nine is quite bitter about how much life asks of them. They feel ill-equipped and devoid of the energy and clarity to provide what is needed. Why exhaust myself physically when someone else is going to just want more from me? Why do the work of making a decision when someone else can choose for both of us? This allows the Nine to confuse their sloth with their ability to accommodate.

Your Encounter with Jesus, the True Peacemaker

Jesus empathizes with the Nine. *Like the Nine, Jesus was unheard by the passive and overpowered by the powerful.* When Jesus visited his hometown, his neighbors were not impressed. They could not see him as anything more than merely "the carpenter's son" (Matthew 13:55). We are told he could do only a few miracles there because of the lack of faith. Throughout his ministry, when Jesus asserted himself boldly, people often became angry with him. After Jesus healed a man on the Sabbath, "the Pharisees and the teachers of the law were furious and began to discuss with one another what they might do to

JESUS, THE TRUE PEACEMAKER

ACCEPTED PEOPLE

RESTED & SLEPT

KNEW HIS PRESENCE MATTERED

OFTEN UNHEARD

PRINCE OF PEACE

BELIEVED CONFLICT WAS VALUABLE

EXERTED HIS ENERGY ON WHAT MATTERED MOST

Jesus" (Luke 6:11). After enough instances of conflict, the religious leaders became so angry that they ultimately conducted a corrupt trial and had him crucified. Their goal was to destroy him. For a fair portion of the trial, Jesus stood in silence, knowing that his words would never change the agendas or outcome of his situation. Jesus understands what it means to be unheard and overpowered.

The Nine also discovers the authority of Jesus and his mastery of living a robust life. *Jesus affirms the True Self of the Nine by accepting people.* After Jesus called the tax collector Matthew to follow him, they went to Matthew's house for dinner. While there, many "questionable" people came by and joined them for food and fellowship. This strange menagerie of friendships caused many of Jesus' fellow Jews to question the company he kept. We're told that the Pharisees asked his disciples, "Why does your teacher eat with tax collectors and sinners?" (Matthew 9:11). Jesus welcomed people as they were. In fact, there isn't a single instance in the gospels where we see Jesus turn someone away who sought him out. Like the Nine, he believed that people should not have to put on a persona to be in his company.

LIKE THE NINE, JESUS WAS UNHEARD BY THE PASSIVE AND OVERPOWERED BY THE POWERFUL.

LIKE THE NINE, JESUS ACCEPTED PEOPLE.

Also like the Nine, Jesus rested and slept. In a story that is quite humorous when you think about it, Jesus and his disciples were out on the sea one day (Mark 4:35–41). Suddenly, a storm came up and the waves began to attack the boat. The disciples became terrified that the boat was going to capsize. Panicked, they turned to Jesus for help.

Consider the scene before them. This was not a luxury yacht with private below-the-deck quarters. This was a basic fishing boat, which meant that Jesus was also exposed to the weather. Wherever he was in the boat, we know he was getting drenched. How was he reacting to a storm powerful enough to flip their boat? He was asleep! This is quite the Nine super move.

Yet Jesus also confronts the False Self of the Nine because he exerted his energy on what mattered most. Jesus chose the better but more difficult path. It would have been so easy for Jesus to spend all of his time with people who were righteous and upstanding. He could have stayed in his hometown and taken up his father's trade as a carpenter. He could have done what I would have done—found a hospitable town in which to set up shop and let the hostile riffraff in the other villages devour themselves. It's not his fault they're all acting like fools. Why bother with such difficult circumstances? Instead, in Luke 5:32, Jesus said, "I have not come to call the righteous, but sinners to repentance." He took action for us. He gave up comfort for love.

Likewise, Jesus believed that conflict was a valuable method of transformation. Though he was known as "the Prince of Peace," Jesus also claimed that he didn't come "to bring peace, but a sword" (Matthew 10:34). He wasn't afraid to confront people. Whether it was his friends, strangers, or influential religious leaders, Jesus was willing to risk being disliked, despised, and even cut off. He simply refused to pretend that life could go on as it was. To bring change, the status quo must be confronted. We often want a Jesus who affirms and consoles us but never confronts us. A story without conflict is boring, and a savior without conflict is a pacifier.

JESUS CONFRONTS THE NINE BY EXERTING HIS ENERGY ON WHAT MATTERED MOST.

How was it possible for Jesus to display such peace and acceptance without ever merging his needs and desires with others or succumbing to the deadly sin of sloth? *Jesus believed his presence mattered to the Father and to others.* Jesus never bought into the lie that God didn't hear him or that God would dismiss him. Though Jesus' friends surely did ignore or overwhelm his voice at times, Jesus never gave up his autonomy. Jesus knew who he was and understood his purpose. In Luke 19:10, he says, "The Son of Man came to seek and to save the lost." His voice mattered. He affirms this in John 5:24: "Whoever hears my word and believes him who sent me has eternal life." Jesus was not forgettable to the people who loved him, and he knew it. To avoid life is to avoid love.

Redeeming Your True Self: From Passive to Present

As the Nine looks back over the story of their life, they're met with difficult memories of being ignored and feeling voiceless. The Nine needs someone to notice them and give them patient, undivided attention. God notices the Nine and stoops to look them in the eyes. As

THE NINE IS GIVEN THE GOOD NEWS, "YOUR PRESENCE MATTERS."

he sits with them in their silence, they become aware that he knows about their fear of losing connection with people, their loss of their voice, and their worship of comfort and sloth. He draws them close. He says to them, *"Your presence matters."* The Nine finds in the gospel the very thing they want—peace in a hostile world.

The Nine is often dismissive of their own importance. In Matthew 13:31–32, Jesus tells an important story for the Nine to remember: "The kingdom of heaven is like a mustard seed, which a man took and planted in his field. Though it is the smallest of all seeds, yet when it grows, it is the largest of garden plants and becomes a tree, so that the birds come and perch in its branches." The redeemed Nine already has the kingdom of God within them, waiting to burst into fullness of life. God has plans for them.

The Nine must relinquish their unrealistic ideas and timeline for peace and replace it with a better peace. The Bible calls this peace *shalom*. In the New Testament, shalom is revealed as the reconciliation of all things to God through the work of Christ. Colossians 1:19–20 tells us, "God was pleased . . . through [Christ] to reconcile to himself all things, whether things on earth or things in heaven, by making peace through [Christ's] blood, shed on the cross." It gives us multidimensional, complete well-being—physical, psychological, social, and spiritual. It results from all of one's relationships being put right. Shalom offers peace with God, peace with others, and peace with oneself. We experience a foretaste of this peace when we walk with God now, and we are promised the fullness of this peace in the new heaven and the new earth that are to come.

What would happen if the Nine believed that their presence was important to others and to God? What if the Holy Spirit were allowed to work his peace down into their souls? With faith that their voice will be heard and valued by God, the Nine can stop feeling the need to passive-aggressively resist or appease people. They can stop trying to fabricate false peace through avoidance and comfort. By trusting that Jesus has brought peace between God and humanity, the Nine no longer needs to live in fear of conflict. Their relationship with ease, passivity, and self-forgetting can be transformed. Jesus gives us peace that is everlasting. The Nine can now choose to follow Jesus on his path to bringing *shalom* and his way of relating to others.

What does it look like to trust him with our relationships and personality?

First, the Nine should survey how sloth has damaged their life. It was wrong that they had to become self-forgetting to survive in this world. It was wrong that they felt they had to dismiss their hopes, dreams, and convictions to keep their relationships intact. Healthy relationships shouldn't require someone to erase themselves. God invites the Nine to bring their grief to him and to their trusted relationships so he can bring healing and consolation. We grieve what has been lost and repent of the damage we've done.

Second, to combat their sloth, the Nine will want to practice the virtue of *exertion*. Life with God is lived by engagement, not by avoidance. Jesus invites the Nine to let go of their sloth and follow him by waking up to their life and asserting themselves. Through physical and mental effort, the Nine can learn to engage their relationships wholeheartedly.

TO COUNTERACT SLOTH, PRACTICE EXERTION.

ENGAGE LIFE WHOLEHEARTEDLY AND DISPLAY FAITH IN THE FORM OF PRIORITIZED ACTION.

The importance of exertion is made clear in the book of James. Listen to all these phrases:

Faith by itself, if it is not accompanied by action, is dead. (2:17)

Show me your faith without deeds, and I will show you my faith by my deeds. (2:18)

As the body without the spirit is dead, so faith without deeds is dead. (2:26)

In other words, the Nine must show their faith in Jesus by *taking action on important matters.*

Good news. Contrary to the Nine's belief that exertion will disrupt their peace, the opposite is actually true. Author Marilyn Vancil (a Nine herself) writes, "Nines experience contentment when they are in harmony with others and when their energy is channeled to a particular calling that makes a significant contribution."[10] The exerted presence of the Nine is a gift to those around them. God will use them to impact other lives.

I know one Nine who stumbled upon a serious car accident. It happened in the middle of a thunderstorm—complete with lightning, wind, and heavy rain. The back of the car was smashed against a tree and the driver wasn't moving. Though the Nine's natural disposition was to assume other people would help, he realized that his CPR and first aid certification made him someone who could make the biggest difference at that moment. He rushed from his car to get to the injured driver, who was in shock and unresponsive. He called 911 and stayed with her to keep her safe until paramedics arrived. His actions helped save her life. He later said, "I realized I could be a man of action. I am capable of making a difference."

By exploring their unresolved anger and dedicating themselves to exertion, the Nine learns to share their opinions, have a redemptive view of conflict, and believe that they have an important role to play in the body of Christ. This virtue can only grow if they believe the good news that God sees them and values their presence and has given them all the grace they need to take risks.

When the Nine practices exertion, their life begins to grow a variety of good fruit. *First, they develop autonomy*—the capacity to be their own person, to live their life according to their own desires and convictions and not someone else's agenda. This does not mean they isolate or disconnect from others. Instead, the Nine learns to resist merging by healthy differentiation. This is the active, ongoing process of defining and revealing themselves, clarifying boundaries, and managing their anxiety that will emerge from risking both greater intimacy and potential separation. They honor their True Self by learning to identify what is going on in their internal world and then expressing that internal world to other people.

Second, they realize the impact they can have on other people's lives. They are just as capable as anyone else of shaping lives, influencing outcomes, and helping people in need. Consciously following Jesus will lead them to become agents of change in their corner of the world.

Third, they experience more vibrancy in their relationship with God and others. By doing the work of showing up, the Nine moves past a hazy fog into a deep connection with God and others. More than just an abstract idea or a worldview, they begin to sense the personhood of God present with them. As they sense God abiding with them at all times, they find the courage and commitment to actively engage their relationships consistently.

Discipleship: Time in Nature and Prayer

To keep themselves from falling back into the enticement of comfort and sloth, the Nine will want to walk with Jesus through spiritual disciplines. The first discipline the Nine will want to practice is one that many already do: *spend time in nature.*[11] Whether walking, cycling, hiking, or swimming, creation reminds us that Christ holds all things together—including us. Though experiencing a life free of conflict is not possible, finding ways to enjoy God's creation can help restore our trust and inner peace.

The second discipline is to *practice fixed-hour prayer.* Throughout the ages, Christians have carried out variations of this. The most common rhythm of this discipline is morning, noon, and evening.

Because the Nine is a creature of habit who also struggles to find mental clarity, the routine of prayer becomes a means by which they can pray themselves into greater clarity. This rhythm creates an opportunity for the quiet voice of God to become clear and for their own heart to awaken to his presence.

Our journey of transformation is unlikely to come easily. We should expect occasional setbacks. The siren song of sloth will likely call out to the Nine—especially when they feel overwhelmed and tired. Remember that this is the False Self trying to drag you back into darkness. But be encouraged. Jesus is at work to set your True Self free. You will have victory. As the Nine walks with Jesus through exerting themselves, they will become more like him. They will experience his peace as it flows through even the most anxious valleys of their soul.

THE NINE REFLECTS GOD'S PEACE & UNITY.

Every person reflects a different aspect of God's character. *The True Self of the Nine reflects God's peace and unity.*[12]

Jesus is clear about those who pursue peace in their life. In Matthew 5:9, he says, "Blessed are the peacemakers, for they will be called children of God." The psalmist says, "Turn from evil and do good; seek peace and pursue it" (34:14). Galatians tells us that peace is a fruit of the Spirit (5:22–23). When the Nine learns to follow Jesus through a balance of peace and exertion, they help us believe that the accepting presence of God is still actively at work in the world and will one day bring us shalom.

Practical Tips for the Nine

1. Practice expressing your opinions and thoughts. You are responsible for making your own decisions. Don't make others live your life for you.

2. **If you don't know what you want, start with what you don't want.** Narrow your options to help give you clarity.

3. **Make a list every day, and do the list.** Create action plans for yourself with goals that are prioritized and specific. Break tasks down into smaller steps.

4. **Be present and engage.** Be aware of your tendency to check out. Acknowledge that your voice and presence matter to the people around you.

5. **Want to know your true feelings? Notice your body language.** Your body knows your feelings before your brain does. What is your body saying?

6. **Move your body.** Physical activity activates more than your body. It also helps your thinking and emotions rouse into life so you can be engaged.

CHAPTER 5

TYPE ONE
THE REFORMER

———●———

Your goodness is a gift from God,
not a reward for your striving.

Before we launched Love Thy Neighborhood, I used to lead a small missions program. There was an empty apartment at a homeless shelter, and the leaders weren't sure what to do with it. I pitched the idea that they should use it as housing for young men who would serve for a year as urban missionaries. I was twenty-five years old, but somehow they entrusted the project to me. Six months later, three guys in their early twenties moved into a homeless shelter voluntarily to live and serve for a year. It felt like a busted-up version of a reality show. Instead of strangers moving in together with a view of beaches and palm trees, our guys had a view of the projects and Happy Liquors. One of those young guys who came to serve was named Jordan.

Jordan had just graduated from college and felt a strong moral conviction to forgo the traditional postgraduation path. Instead of the "get a decent-paying job so you won't end up homeless" route, Jordan opted for the "get a job that essentially pays nothing and live with the homeless" route. Jordan quickly gained and maintained a reputation for being a hard worker who approached each task with the highest excellence. He always clocked in right on time and often worked late. He never skipped any appointments or cut corners on his responsibilities. On the rare occasion that he made a mistake, he was known for finding his supervisor and making them aware before they even had the chance to discover it.

The residents at our facility were men with a mixture of those with a history of mental illness and of addiction. Most came to us because they had been homeless and needed help. These are the men Jordan came to serve. Every week, Jordan would cook them meals, teach the Bible, pray with them, and organize group activities. When he taught, he spoke with conviction about God's truth but also with compassion. If something was unethical, unjust, or unmerciful, I could depend on Jordan to bring it to my attention, along with a gentle suggestion about how to fix the problem. Though he could have eaten most of his meals in his apartment, Jordan almost always opted to eat with the guys in the recovery program—an outward reflection of his inner conviction that being with the men as much as possible was the right thing to do.

Today, Jordan and his family live in a third-world country where he continues to help transform lives hurt by brokenness. If you're highly ethical, honest, hardworking, and dedicated to changing the world like Jordan, you may be a One.

True Self

When healthy, the One is known as the most overtly ethical voice among all the types. They're activists, teachers, missionaries, and crusaders who want to improve the world. Keenly sensitive to issues of fairness and justice, they're concerned with both *doing good*

and *being good*. They don't want
to wake up one day and realize
they're the "whitewashed tombs"
Jesus referred to—perfect on the
outside and corrupt on the inside
(Matthew 23:27–28). Because the
One tends to focus on instituting
and defending goodness, they are

orderly people who tend to be methodical and systematic.

Motivated by their desire to be honest, they don't tend to spin
the truth or deceive. They speak factually. To ensure they have
stated all the facts and to satisfy their need to justify their actions,
they also sometimes talk at length. If you've ever been caught in a
One's MRM (moral rationale monologue), you know it can take a
while for them to thoroughly explain things. Because the One is
not influenced by personal feelings or opinions in considering and
representing facts, they have the ability to make excellent judgments and can be quite objective. Their goal is to remain unbiased
in the service of truth, justice, and fairness.

The healthy One is highly disciplined. Not surprisingly, most
Ones I know are early risers, and many follow a strict exercise and
diet regimen. Likewise, many Ones I know do quiet time, Bible
study, and prayer on a daily basis. I heard about a One who wakes
up every day at five in the morning to do a one-hour workout on
their elliptical . . . while studying the Bible at the same time.

They are often intense—especially about issues of ethics. If the
right (or wrong?) topic is mentioned, a One can quickly switch
from a water pistol to a machine gun. Their convictions are deep
and strong. Because they see themselves as stewards of the time,
money, and life that has been entrusted to them, they are typically
hardworking and diligent.

When the One is healthy, they bring their desire for reformation and growth to their faith. They are often concerned with both

personal righteousness and societal justice. In prayer they typically confess their sins with integrity and frequently pray for others who are in pain or suffering injustice. They see the gap between what *is* and what *can be*, but they trust in God's unfolding plan with a relaxed confidence, knowing he will complete his good work at the perfect time.

False Self

When the One is unhealthy, they overidentify with improving themselves and the world. Their pursuit of improvement turns into criticism. They develop an inner critic that judges all of their

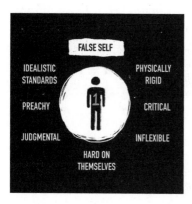

thoughts and actions—making them increasingly rigid from the guilt and anger they feel inside. This voice is often cruel and belittling to them while remaining quiet enough to go undetected by the One.

As they are abused by their inner critic, the One's internal emotional experience pours out onto others, who experience them as judgmental, critical, and harsh. Just as the One expects more out of themselves, they also expect more out of the world. They can become inflexible, micromanaging, and controlling. Becoming overly attached to their (sometimes arbitrary) ideas of right and wrong, they can be stubborn and uncompromising. As they encounter flaws they can't seem to fix (their own, other's, nature's, the universe's), their anger and resentment grow. No matter how hard they try, somewhere in the world there are still dishes in the sink and floors unswept.

A lifetime of being hard on themselves results in the One

becoming physically stiff when they're upset or uncertain. Because their body has a difficult time relaxing, the body language of the One can sometimes communicate to others that they are being evaluated or judged.

When they're unhealthy, the One brings their judgments into their church communities. Is everyone reading their Bible every day? How long? Which translation? Are they doctrinally pure? Why didn't the pastor mention those other five verses that correspond to the text? They can become the sin police, always on the lookout for infractions and people in need of correction. Their tenacious criticism and pessimism can smother the aroma of grace that is central to the Christian life. The inner critic of the One often commandeers Bible verses and religious language. It may use God's words, but it doesn't have his voice. While it may have his intensity and conviction, it lacks his compassion and grace. Far before anyone else is beaten up by the One's inner critic, they fall victim to it first.

Childhood and Adolescence: Conditional Love and Criticism

The childhood theme of the One is *conditional love and criticism.* Many Ones come from backgrounds with either too much structure or not enough. On the one side, you can imagine kids of pastors or missionaries, military brats, or kids whose parents would never allow burping at the dinner table. There were simply too many rules and unreal-

THE CHILDHOOD THEME OF THE ONE IS CONDITIONAL LOVE & CRITICISM.

istic expectations for their small shoulders. When the One made mistakes (and they did . . . because they were a *child*), they were criticized and corrected—often with more harshness than necessary.

On the flip side are Ones who come from backgrounds where they were not given adequate structure. In these homes, issues such as trauma, mental illness, or substance abuse may have created a chaotic home. They lacked routines, clear expectations, or a dependable moral ethic. They learned to be their own caretaker by becoming hyper-responsible, acting in accordance with moral standards, and punishing themselves when needed. Because no one else would do it, the One decided they would just have to parent themselves.

Surprisingly, they found that when they did perform correctly, they were showered with praise and love. Pavlov's dogs associated ringing a bell with getting fed. The One linked following the rules with being loved. If a little bit of good could get them a little bit of love, then surely a lot of good would get them a lot of love. So the One set out to become the very best at being very good. They developed an internal parental voice to protect them from making mistakes, which then developed into an inner critic that evaluates them daily. Now the One feels like they're always on trial.

These experiences of conditional love and criticism led to the conclusion that *it's not okay to be wrong or make mistakes.*[1] As opposed to seeing mistakes as a natural part of learning and growing, the One experiences mistakes as condemnation and confirmation of their corruption. The One comes to believe this so profoundly that they begin to believe they should punish themselves, regardless of whether anyone else does. By punishing themselves for their mistakes, they hope no one else will have to. If you've ever been around a One who seems to have arbitrary rules, this is why. It's better to have *too many rules* and be right than *not enough rules* and be wrong. Why put one padlock on a door when you can put five?

This leaves the One *afraid of being bad, corrupt, evil, or defective.*[2] They became scared that they will never pass their internal tests, meet their standards, or truly become decent people. Because being wrong requires punishment, the One became afraid that they were trapped in a life in which they had no moral choice but to punish themselves endlessly. Likewise, they became scared that others saw them as bad people who were selfish, sinful, and deficient. Indeed, their fear is confirmed in Romans 3:23: "All have sinned and fall short of the glory of God." Tragically, they can't see that their existence is good even when their sin is bad.

If you take a kid and inject them full of feelings of conditional love, criticism, a hatred of mistakes, and a fear that they may be morally bankrupt and evil, you end up with someone who feels a lot of *anger and guilt*.[3] While the One believes that open displays of anger toward others is typically unacceptable, they often feel that anger turned inward at themselves is not just acceptable but deserved. Underneath that anger is guilt. Of all the types in the Body Triad, the One is the most aware of their feelings of guilt. Whereas the Eight denies their guilt and the Nine numbs their guilt, the One absorbs not only their *true guilt* but their *false guilt* as well. They feel guilty not only for the things they are morally responsible for but also for the things they are not. Just in case Jesus' death wasn't enough punishment for their sins, they opt to punish themselves too.

Behind their earnest, striving exterior is just a kid who wants someone to see them just as they are and tell them, *"You are good."*[4] They long to know they can stop striving for some unrealistic ideal because they already possess what they've been looking for—the truth that their relational presence is inherently valuable. The One internalized the idea that only bad people want credit for things you're supposed to do. Of course, kids end up believing the messages they hear the most often. If their good behavior typically goes unnoticed but their bad behavior gets a lot of attention, a kid will end up believing most people in their life think they're a bad person.

Here's what the One wants more than anything else in life: *to have integrity*.[5] They want to be honest and live out their principles. The One wants to be whole and undivided. Author Donald Miller says that integrity is "a soul fully integrated, no difference between his act and his actual person. Having integrity is about being the

THE ONE WANTS TO HAVE INTEGRITY.

same person on the inside that we are on the outside."[6] The One longs for structural integrity for their soul. They want to fulfill the purpose they were designed for without collapsing because of their own flaws. In a world that is deformed and fallen, they want to be agents of reformation, architects of honor, and laborers of righteousness.

Sadly, this good desire for integrity gets twisted and becomes something altogether different.

Nurturing Your False Self: Mistaking Perfectionism for Integrity

WHAT IS THE ONE WILLING TO SACRIFICE?

THE IDOL OF THE ONE: PERFECTIONISM

The One settles for the false idol of perfectionism. The truth is that the One can't tell the difference between integrity and perfectionism. Being perfect offers a solution to being bad, wrong, or criticized. This idol calls the One to keep trying harder, to refine more, to push and chisel and strive. By focusing their energy on perfection, the One subconsciously believes they will silence the critical inner voice that relentlessly interrogates them. This sets up an all-or-nothing game: be perfect or fail. If I felt that much pressure all the time, I'd be a little tightly wound and anxious too.

The idol of perfectionism requires sacrifices. It requires them to sacrifice fun and spontaneity, their own desires and wants, and giving and receiving grace. Grace is too gentle, too compassionate, too lenient in its approach. Surely the discipline of perfectionism is a better cure for the flaws of the world.

What happens when the One puts their hope in perfectionism? They grow the deadly sin of *resentment*.[7] Strong feelings of displeasure and annoyance at the faults that deform creation begin to surge within the One. Frustration sizzles like a low-grade fever under the surface as the One lives with the sense that things are not as they should be. This anger is different from the forceful anger of other types. The One attempts to filter their anger through their perfectionism and ethics, making it more controlled and subdued. Imagine someone forcing a smile but their eye is twitching. Periodically their pressurized irritation builds until the full force of their anger finally explodes.

HOW DOES THE ONE NURTURE THEIR DEADLY SIN?

MUSTS, OUGHTS & SHOULDS

CRITICIZING THEMSELVES & OTHERS

RESENTMENT

GOOD DEEDS

BEING IN CONTROL

As the old saying goes, "Resentment is like drinking poison and waiting for the other person to die." The problem here is that the One is just as resentful of themselves as everyone else. Though the One is angry because they are failing to live up to their own ideals, they can only beat themselves up for so long before they need relief. That relief often comes in the form of directing their inner critic outward at others. Judging others allows the One to feel some momentary alleviation from their own failures. ("At least I'm not as bad as *that* guy!") Unlike helpful anger, which responds to injustice adequately and protects us from danger before quickly dissipating, resentment doesn't go away. It fosters mistrust and keeps records of wrongs to be used when needed. Healthy anger is a quick, strategic punch. Resentment is a choke hold.

To cope with their fear of being bad, corrupt, evil, or defective and to protect their idol of perfectionism, the One defends themselves through *reaction formation*[8]—a defense mechanism by which individuals do the opposite of their true instincts. ("I want to do X, so I'd better do Y instead.") When the One experiences what they deem as "unacceptable" feelings or desires, reaction formation will concede to their inner critic, which dictates what is acceptable based on social protocol, contextual expectations, or moral principles. In this way, the One learns to ignore their desires. I can't count the number of times through the years I've heard pastors say, "I told God I never wanted to be a pastor, so I *knew* he must have been calling me to be a pastor." Either God really enjoys forcing people to do things they hate or there are a lot of Ones in the pastorate.

As a child, the One felt they could never measure up to the ideal, never rest, never fulfill all of their obligations and duties. No matter how hard they ran on the treadmill and no matter how perfect their form was, eventually they always fell. For whatever reason, they could never hold on to the words of encouragement about their efforts (or perhaps those words were never given), but the criticisms stuck with them. However the label of "BAD" got there, the One has been trying to furiously remove it. They don't want to be defective. They want to be good. The problem is we can't beat ourselves into perfect form.

Each type finds their deadly sin familiar and defensible. *The One believes the failures of others (and their own failure too) justifies their resentment.* This resentment allows them to be above others morally. It makes other people take moral failure seriously and ensures that the One does not give up on their own efforts at bettering themselves. By being angry with themselves, they believe one day they'll reach their goal of being good.

Your Encounter with Jesus, the True Reformer

As the One encounters Jesus, they find someone who empathizes with their pain. *Like the One, Jesus was criticized and the love people gave him was conditional.* People offered fickle affection when he behaved like the Messiah they wanted. They offered scorn when he didn't. The religious leaders (aka, the *most* moral people) were the worst of all. By the time Jesus began his ministry, the Pharisees had developed a system of 613 laws that they expected Jesus

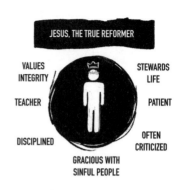

JESUS, THE TRUE REFORMER

VALUES INTEGRITY

STEWARDS LIFE

TEACHER

PATIENT

DISCIPLINED

OFTEN CRITICIZED

GRACIOUS WITH SINFUL PEOPLE

to follow. The religious leaders ignored his good deeds, deciding instead to criticize, find fault, set traps, and twist his words. In exasperation, Jesus eventually responded by exclaiming, "Woe to you, because you load people down with burdens they can hardly carry, and you yourselves will not lift one finger to help them" (Luke 11:46). Jesus—who was in every sense *truly good*—was told all the time that he was bad. Jesus understands the pain of the One. He knows what it's like to live under the weight of criticism and conditional love.

The One also discovers that Jesus reveals his authority and shows why he is a model to trust and follow. *Jesus affirms the True Self of the One by valuing integrity.* Throughout the Sermon on the Mount, Jesus redirects the attention of his listeners beyond man-made rules toward true righteousness. This new calling breaks the yoke of arbitrary laws and yet also raises the bar. He calls them to change not just their behavior but also their hearts. "Be perfect, therefore, as your heavenly Father is perfect" (Matthew 5:48). This verse can easily trip up the One. ("See?! Jesus *wants* me to pursue perfection!") Enneagram teacher Ian Morgan Cron interviewed a seminary

LIKE THE ONE, JESUS STEWARDED HIS LIFE.

student (who also happened to be a One) who shared that the Greek word for "perfect" here shouldn't be understood as flawlessness so much as wholeness. She said that Jesus meant "perfect" in the sense of "the end for which you were created, rather than conforming to an ideal."[9] Jesus calls the One to live for the end for which they were created. Be whole as God is whole. That is integrity, and Jesus affirms it.

Also like the One, Jesus stewarded his life. We see him traveling, mentoring, teaching, and healing. He was clearly someone who studied diligently and must have read frequently to memorize the Scriptures. Before he began his ministry, we are told he was a carpenter. He likely worked under his father, Joseph, to build or fix local farming equipment. Jesus never gave any impression of being frivolous or careless. Jesus' value of stewardship was clear in the parable of the bags of gold—a story that illustrates how we are put on earth to work (Matthew 25:14–30). This is why the apostle Paul later spent so much time reminding believers that we belong to Christ and owe him our allegiance. Our life is not ours alone but a gift with which we have been entrusted. Pastor Rick Warren writes, "Time is your most precious gift because you only have a set amount of it. You can make more money, but you can't make more time."[10] Jesus was intentional with his time.

However, Jesus also confronts the False Self of the One because he was gracious with sinful people. When Peter asked how many times he should forgive someone who sins against him, Jesus told him to forgive them *every* time (Matthew 18:21–22). In the Sermon on the Mount, he tells his listeners, "For if you forgive other people when they sin against you, your heavenly Father will also forgive you. But if you do not forgive others their sins,

JESUS CONFRONTS THE ONE BY BEING GRACIOUS WITH SINFUL PEOPLE.

your Father will not forgive your sins" (Matthew 6:14–15). When the woman caught in adultery was brought before Jesus, he protected her from her accusers and offered a message of grace to her before calling her to righteousness. "'Then neither do I condemn you,' Jesus declared. 'Go now and leave your life of sin'" (John 8:11). (Please, take note of the order here: grace first, truth second.) Jesus was gracious to sinners (see Matthew 26:28; Luke 23:34). As pastor Dane Ortlund has observed, "When Jesus Christ sees the fallenness of the world all about him, his deepest impulse, his most natural instinct, is to move toward that sin and suffering, not away from it."[11]

Jesus was patient with God's unfolding plan. It is a strange but beautiful thing that Jesus, who is divine, would choose not to control every outcome. The mere idea that there are thousands of unmade beds around the world is enough to make some Ones want to lead a coup. Though Jesus could easily have become bitter and rigid at the corruption of the world and seized control, he chose to trust his Father. In Matthew 24, Jesus talks about his eventual return. For all the clarity and conviction he has, he suddenly shares this surprising statement: "But about that day or hour no one knows, not even the angels in heaven, nor the Son, but only the Father" (v. 36). He doesn't seem to press the Father for answers or to demand that all things be restored instantly. He simply trusts that the Father knows what he is doing and that all will be made well at the right time.

How did he do this? How was it possible for Jesus to display such integrity and conviction without becoming an obsessive rule follower or succumbing to the deadly sin of resentment? *Jesus believed that the Father knew he was good.* The apostle Peter calls Jesus "a lamb without blemish or defect" (1 Peter 1:19). The apostle John tells us that "in him is no sin" (1 John 3:5). In every way, Jesus manifests and upholds all that is good. The Father looks on Jesus and sees a pure reflection of his own goodness. His existence brings the Father pleasure.

Redeeming Your True Self: From Perfectionism to Patience

Life has been difficult for the One. They've tried to be good in a world gone bad. God doesn't look at them and say, "Would you just relax already?" God has mercy for them. The One needs someone to find them in their greatest moment of guilt, in their angst among

THE ONE IS GIVEN THE GOOD NEWS,
"I HAVE MADE YOU GOOD JUST AS YOU ARE."

a broken world, in the moment they gave up the playfulness of their youth for the seriousness of adulthood. God sees the One and kneels to look them in the eyes. He appreciates their desire for righteousness and justice, their desire to free themselves from sin, and their eagerness to help fix the brokenness of the world. He knows about their fear of being bad, evil, corrupt, or defective, about their idol of perfectionism and their deadly sin of resentment. Knowing they cannot save themselves, Jesus engulfs them in his perfect embrace. In purity, spotlessness, and truth, God says to the One, *"I have made you good, just as you are."* The One finds in the gospel the promise that their integrity will be whole and faultless. Jesus invites the One to see the goodness of their existence and invites them to receive his blamelessness.

First, God has given the One the goodness of their existence. They bear the image of God and carry an inherent dignity within them. Valued by God, they are crafted to share in his relational nature. Like God, they think, feel, and act. As part of God's creation, he still declares, "It is good," over them. The fact that the One exists gives pleasure to God. Even the worst sinner bears this aspect of goodness. We may despise our existence, but God doesn't. We are not a mistake.

Second, God has given the One the goodness of Jesus. Through his life, death, and resurrection, Jesus has made the One good, just as they are. As a donor can cover debts, as a blanket can cover cold, as a hen covers her chicks, so Jesus covers sin. The letter of Jude describes Jesus' act of bringing the One before God the Father: "to present you before his glorious presence without fault and with great joy" (v. 24). Not only does God give them the righteousness of Jesus, but he promises that their life will bear increasingly good fruit as the years pass!

How can the One respond to the good news that God has made them good just as they are? To counteract their bitterness, *they can practice patience.*[12] Jesus calls the One to grow in their capacity to tolerate the existence of sin, flaws, and delays without becoming bitter. Patience requires the One to accept the conditions and pace of life's circumstances. In Luke 8:15, Jesus shares the parable of the sower, where he says to his listeners, "The seed on good soil stands for those with a noble and good heart, who hear the word, retain it, and by persevering produce a crop." The English Standard Version renders the last phrase as "bear fruit with patience." The image here is to "patiently persevere." Implicit in Jesus' farming metaphor is this: growing fruit takes time.

TO COUNTERACT RESENTMENT, PRACTICE PATIENCE.

TOLERATE IMPERFECTIONS AND TRUST GOD'S UNFOLDING PLAN AND TIMING.

Enneagram teacher and author Richard Rohr says, "If we do not transform our pain, we will most assuredly transmit it."[13] The One often transmits their pain as bitterness. Jesus does not ask the One to give up their anger but to shape it into a righteous anger at injustice. In order to wield anger correctly, the One must uncover and process the roots of their anger. By doing so, they can release their bitterness and come to appreciate that God's plan is still unfolding. When their ideals are not met, the One is invited to receive the peace of Christ and accept the reality of their situation. The One would do well to take some advice from some of Jesus' favorite people—namely, alcoholics. Many pray the Serenity Prayer on the hour throughout their journey to recovery: "God, grant me the serenity to accept the things I cannot change, the courage to change the things I can, and the wisdom to know the difference." Excavate your bitterness. Practice patience.

I know a One who was slandered and lost his longtime job as a result. In his earlier years, his resentment would have made this situation unbearable. Now an older man, he refused to speak ill of his accusers and instead chose to lavishly love them through acts of kindness and words of affirmation. It was astounding to watch. He decided that God would sort out the injustice of it all and that his calling was to love his enemies and pray for them. This is patience in action.

When the One practices patience, their life begins to grow a variety of good fruit. *First, practicing patience allows the One to enjoy the experience of grace.* They become more aware of the unmerited favor of God. Unlike judgment, which is never content no matter how high a mountain you climb, grace is like water flowing to the bottom of the valley. It meets you at your lowest. A One who experiences grace becomes a One who loves to give grace.

Second, practicing patience quiets the inner critic. Donald Miller writes, "If we hear, in our inner ear, a voice saying we are failures, we are losers, we will never amount to anything, this is the voice of Satan trying to convince the bride that the groom does not love her. This is not the voice of God. God woos us with kindness."[14] God wants to replace the voice of the judgmental inner critic with the kind and patient voice of the Holy Spirit.

Third, practicing patience will bring joy and fun back into their life. Patience lets the One lay down their tools of self-flagellation. Though joy, fun, and relaxation are all separate things, they certainly have a relationship with one another. The author of Ecclesiastes reminds us, "A person can do nothing better than to eat and drink and find satisfaction in their own toil. This too, I see, is from the hand of God, for without him, who can eat or find enjoyment?" (2:24–25).

Discipleship: Nature and Journaling

To protect themselves from falling back into their old way of life, the One will want to walk with Jesus through spiritual disciplines.[15] Two disciplines in particular will help the One. *The first discipline the One will want to practice is taking regular walks in nature.* Being in nature turns the One's attention away from their bitterness and instead focuses it on something grander. It pulls them out of their judgment and criticism into a space that can be appreciated just as it is. Nature displays the steady works of God and irrefutable evidence of his unfolding plan. Just as God faithfully tends to nature, he will tend to the needs of the world.

Second, the One will want to practice journaling. Journaling will help the One develop candid honesty. As pastor and Enneagram author AJ Sherrill writes, "To verbally articulate imperfection is difficult, but to record imperfection on paper can be emotionally painful. When we write out the cries of the heart, it can feel more official and somehow truer than if it remains in our head. Therefore, it is easy to understand why journaling would be difficult, particularly for Ones."[16] We can only come to trust that God tenderly cares for our imperfections by bringing them to him.

Change is slower (and maybe far more irritating) than we'd prefer. Our False Self will fight back.[17] But remember that Jesus is faithful, and he will set our True Self free. As the One

THE ONE REFLECTS GOD'S GOODNESS & RIGHTNESS.

walks with Jesus, pursuing both integrity and patience, they will become more like their Teacher.

Each of the traits of the Enneagram—when healthy—reflect a different aspect of God's character. *The True Self of the One reflects God's goodness and rightness.*[18] With Jesus patiently guiding them, the One can help the world see that God is still at work to bring transformation. Having grown in their patience and acceptance of God's timeline and unfolding plan, the One is free to pursue transformation and improvement without pushiness or harsh judgment. This mixture of grace and truth is the aroma of Jesus drawing broken lives into the arms of God, where they can be saved and healed.

Practical Tips for the One

1. Have realistic expectations of yourself and others. Everyone has flaws and limitations. Unrealistic expectations are just premeditated resentment.
2. Give yourself permission to make mistakes. God's grace covers your weaknesses, your flaws, and your sins. He doesn't need you to be perfect.
3. Have a conversation with your inner critic. This voice is not the voice of God. To be less critical of others, you have to be less critical of yourself. Be kind to yourself.
4. Catch yourself criticizing. It's easy to spot the flaws and shortcomings. The harder work is to withhold judgment and focus on the good.
5. Notice the good and express appreciation. Be lavish with your praise and gratitude. This will build bonds in your relationships and kick-start your joy.
6. Spend time each day doing activities you enjoy. Remember, dismissing pleasure won't help you in the long term. Invest energy into pleasure.

THE HEART TRIAD
Searching for Identity

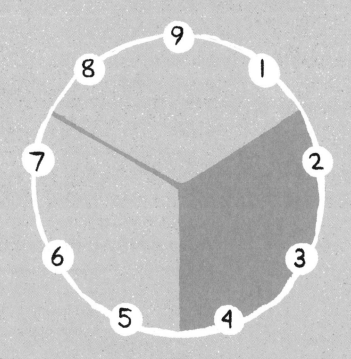

CHAPTER 6

TYPE TWO
THE HELPER

———•———

God wants you for who you
are, not what you give.

A couple of years ago, I got the flu—the worst flu I've ever had. I ended up being stuck in bed for more than a week. I didn't leave my house for eight days. It was miserable. As I lay in bed drifting in and out of consciousness, I got texts from three different people:

> "I LEFT SOME OF YOUR FAVORITE CANDY ON YOUR FRONT PORCH. FEEL BETTER SOON!"

> "I FOUND THIS MEDICINE THAT'S SUPPOSED TO HELP YOU GET BETTER FASTER. I'M GOING TO GET YOU SOME ON MY LUNCH BREAK."

> "I PICKED UP SOME CANDY AND MEDICINE FOR YOU. I'M ON THE WAY OVER TO DROP IT OFF."

It was amazing, and I was grateful to have people take such good care of me. What do these folks have in common?

All three of these people are Enneagram Twos.

True Self

When they're healthy and flourishing, the Two uses their gifts to serve others and care for people in need. As a member of the Heart Triad, the Two has their heart dialed in on their relationships and has an uncanny X-ray-like vision that can perceive the needs of those around them. Highly attentive, perceptive, and responsive, they are frequently proactive about the needs of others without being prompted. Helpful, warm, and encouraging, the Two is a natural befriender—making both their inner circle and strangers feel welcome and loved.

The Two is capable of extraordinary sacrifice. If you had a finger cut off in some freak accident, they'd probably ask the doctor if they could donate one of theirs to help you out. Many Twos find more pleasure in giving than receiving. If you ask a Two about the purpose of life, many of them would say, "It's to be generous."

The Two is all about love in action. When they see someone in need, they often well up with compassion and feel a desire to put on some scrubs and start caring for people. Their tender hearts and emotional attunement allow them to empathize with the pain of others. This is why we all want a Two around when we're hurting. They make amazing friends and companions when we're stumbling to the bathroom in our bathrobe, holding a bucket of vomit, wondering if today will be the end of us. They've probably memorized which of the five love languages is your top choice, as well as your favorite drink from the coffee shop.

The Two experiences a special connection with God when they unconditionally serve others. The pain of the world affects them emotionally and they are moved to take compassionate action. The vibrant Two experiences friendship with God and enjoys life *with* him, not just life *for* him. They slow down enough to be at peace with the God who loves them as they are, and they are happy to receive his generous love without attempting to earn it.

False Self

When the Two becomes unhealthy, they overidentify with helping others. They need to be needed. Identifying and responding to the needs of others becomes less about the other person and more about their own insecurity. By serving other people, the Two hopes to earn and hold on to love. They take their good gift of helping and supercharge it. When this happens, being helpful isn't part of who they are; it becomes the whole picture. They're haunted by the question, "Who am I if I'm not needed?"

I remember watching a comedy where a mother wanders an empty house, unsure of what to do with herself because her husband and older children are all gone. Finally, she creeps into her baby's nursery, where she finds her daughter asleep. After looking lovingly at her dozing infant, she reaches down and begins to poke her harder and harder until suddenly the baby wakes up crying. The mother scoops her daughter into her arms and says, "Oh, there, there!" and begins to console her.[1]

If a Two is not careful, they seek out people with massive needs (such as addicts or narcissists) to fill their own emptiness. They end up providing 24-7 service for adults who have the emotional maturity of a middle schooler. This codependency leaves them feeling needed (which gives them purpose) but also feeling used (which leaves them bitter).

A trait that can surprise others is the anger of the Two. When they feel unappreciated or taken for granted, the Two can suddenly transform from warm and affable to cold and hostile. If left unaddressed, this anger may grow into resentment, at which time the Two abandons the relationship in favor of people who are more appreciative of their generosity.

When they are on autopilot, the Two becomes a people pleaser. They lose touch with their own wants and needs as they overly accommodate requests from other people. As a result, they struggle with boundaries. Once they lose track of their own boundaries, they also lose track of the boundaries of others. They become intrusive and begin to display a subtle form of arrogance that assumes other people need them to survive. Because the needs of others define their own sense of self-worth, they become possessive of their relationships and can be jealous or resentful when they are no longer central to another person's life.

When their thirst for being appreciated goes unchecked, the Two can develop a relationship with God that revolves exclusively around service. They'll serve God until they've wrung every drop of energy out of their muscles, yet they'll refuse to receive from him. Asking others for help (including asking God) feels selfish. They believe their value comes only in terms of how well they serve. Likewise, because they do serve so well, they can come to believe that God owes them. When they feel their service is not appreciated by God or that God is not responding as they have asked him to, they can grow bitter toward him as well. They are left longing to be loved for who they are, not what they do.

Childhood and Adolescence: Neglect and Unfulfilled Needs

While the truth is that everyone has some level of unmet needs in their childhood, for the Two, *neglect and unfulfilled needs* is so prominent it becomes a theme. The Two's own needs were often the first thing sacrificed in favor of the community. In some cases, there was an early awareness of the limitations or unreliability of

THE CHILDHOOD THEME OF THE TWO IS NEGLECT & UNFULFILLED NEEDS.

their caretakers (instability, mental health issues, addiction, job loss, lack of presence). To survive, the young Two filled the gap left by their unreliable caretakers by becoming motherly or fatherly themselves. In other cases, someone in the family had significant needs (physical, emotional, or mental disabilities), where the Two was assigned the role of helping care for those needs.

After our parents divorced when I was still in diapers, my older sister became my constant caretaker as we shuffled back and forth between two houses. Through the years, she often made sure I had my backpack or my clothes or that each parent was kept up-to-date on important news about me. People used to joke that my sister was my second mother. No surprise that she eventually came out a Two. In many ways, she had to grow up faster than kids should. In the process, her own needs were often pushed aside.

Being surrounded by so much need, the last thing the Two wanted to do was add to the burden. Somewhere deep in the subconscious of that little kid, a belief began to form: *"It's not okay to have your own needs."*[2] Needs are selfish, inconsiderate, embarrassing things that don't deserve love or care. Other people are allowed to be needy, but the Two is not. Always be the nurse, never the patient.

Why can other people ask for what they need? Because they're valuable. Why can other people receive help when they need it? Because they're loved. Twos believed their own needs were irrelevant and a burden to others, and they became *afraid of being unworthy of love.*[3] We can't assume that the miracle of being a living, breathing human being means we're worthy of people's attention or adoration—at least that feels true for the Two themselves.

Take a kid who is scared they aren't worthy of love and always praised for their sacrificial service, and then afflict them with *having needs* (God forbid!), and you've got someone who is going to feel a lot of *shame.*[4] The problem with being praised for always putting our own needs last is that eventually we think we *deserve* to always be last. Many Twos wrestle with the question, "Shouldn't I *want* to be last?" Even the Scriptures tell us that "the last will be first" (Matthew 20:16). One of the biggest triggers of shame for a Two is having needs and asking other people for help.

Behind all of their sacrifices and service is just a kid who wants to be cherished and have someone tell them, *"You are loved and wanted for who you are, not what you do."*[5] They want to know their value isn't tied to their acts of service. The Two longs to know that

THE TWO WANTS TO BE LOVED & CHERISHED UNCONDITIONALLY.

they are worthy of love and adoration, not because they earned it, but because someone has decided they are worthy of it.

What do they want more than anything else in life? The Two wants *to be cherished and loved unconditionally.*[6] Their heart aches to know that someone notices them hidden in the midst of the crowd and finds their nonserving, nonperforming, just-as-they-are presence pleasurable and wonderful. After always being the last in line in the world, they long to be the first in someone's heart.

However, somewhere outside of their conscious thought, this beautiful desire to be cherished gets warped into something harmful. This is where their story really takes a turn.

Nurturing Your False Self: Mistaking Being Indispensable with Being Cherished

Years ago, when I worked at the homeless shelter, we were trying to decide whether to paint our brick building to give it an updated look. An interior designer came out and said, "Once you do this, it's permanent. You can't go backward. You will always have to paint this building. You'll be dependent on paint forever."

In many ways, the Two makes this same mistake. Since they can't find someone who will love and cherish them unconditionally, the Two *settles for the false idol of being indispensable.* They paint themselves into the lives of others. The truth is that the Two often can't tell the difference between being cherished and being indispensable. Being treasured and being needed feel the same. The Two feels relationally safe when they're needed, so they create situations where they're needed. If someone is *needed*, they cannot be *abandoned*. So, the Two has an answer to the question, "Who am I?" It's, "I am indispensable."

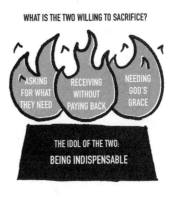

WHAT IS THE TWO WILLING TO SACRIFICE?

ASKING FOR WHAT THEY NEED

RECEIVING WITHOUT PAYING BACK

NEEDING GOD'S GRACE

THE IDOL OF THE TWO: BEING INDISPENSABLE

However, being indispensable requires some heavy sacrifices. The Two must sacrifice asking for what they need, receiving from others without feeling compelled to pay them back, and receiving God's grace. I don't mean that God doesn't have grace for them; I mean that they sacrifice *experiencing* it. Grace is built on the assumption that we have needs. Grace lets us show up as a hot mess, with broken bones, shattered egos, and bad breath. It's hard to admit we need to be saved when we're busy saving everyone around us.

What happens when the Two puts their hope and identity into being indispensable? They grow the deadly sin of *pride*.[7] This type of pride isn't bold self-flattery or cocky arrogance. They aren't throwing a parade for themselves. It's pride with a twist. They're the most sacrificial, the most generous, the most helpful. They're the lowliest servant and actively competing for the award of "Most Humble"—and in their mind, they are winning. As C. S. Lewis has written, "Pride gets no pleasure out of having something, only out of having more of it than the next man . . . It is the comparison that makes you proud: the pleasure of being above the rest."[8] This is what makes this sin so deadly—it's pride disguising itself as humility.

HOW DOES THE TWO NURTURE
THEIR DEADLY SIN?

ALWAYS ACCOMODATING OTHERS
ABUNDANT COMPLIMENTS
PRIDE
HELPFUL DEEDS
PERSONAL SACRIFICES

Unlike true humility, which has an accurate view of one's needs, abilities, and importance, pride blinds us from seeing the truth. This is why so many Twos lack boundaries. Pride has no interest in setting realistic limits in relationships. It's Overestimating 101—overestimating our capacities, our resources, our importance. Denying our needs and limits doesn't make us more lovable; it just makes us irrational and a bit delusional.[9]

To cope with neglect and unfulfilled needs and maintain their self-image of being indispensable, the Two defends themselves through *repression*[10]—a defense mechanism by which individuals are unaware of their own needs and desires. They shut away all their preferences, longings, and boundaries. If you ask a Two what they need, they're likely to respond with, "I don't need anything. Do *you* need anything?" Of course, we can't truly vanquish our needs. Instead, the Two actually projects their unmet needs onto others. They give to others what they wish others would give them to them. (Yet they also refuse to receive from others. What a quandary!) They then bury their pride alongside their needs, where it operates undetected.

A Two told me a story about taking a late-night road trip with her sister who had fallen asleep. This Two was so exhausted she began to doze off at the wheel. She knew she couldn't keep going, but she refused to wake her sister up to ask her to drive. Simultaneously, she was bitter toward her sister for not being awake and offering to drive. (In her sister's defense, it's hard to know what someone needs when they don't tell you . . . or when you're asleep.) Years later, this Two admitted that asking for help—even when she could have killed everyone in the car—didn't feel like a realistic option. "It was ridiculous. We could have died, but I just couldn't bring myself to admit I needed help." Don't underestimate how far down a Two can bury their own needs.

Here's the truth of it: As children, the Two poured themselves out for others. Whether Mom left them in charge when she drank too much or Dad worked too much, thus leaving the household in need, or whether a sibling with special needs needed extra care or the other kids in the orphanage needed a mother figure, the Two learned that their place in the world was to serve the needs of others. Whether they meant to or not, the people in their life praised them for being self-forgetting and sacrificial. That little kid learned that they received adoration from others through helping. They learned to stuff their desires and needs away, believing people would love them less if they were to express them. You can't blame a kid for becoming hooked on the thing that gave them the most consistent affection from the people around them. The problem is that helping others is supposed to be a byproduct of love, not a method to earn it.

Remember, each type's sin is referred to as "deadly" because it feels so familiar that it's almost comforting. In light of our life story, our deadly sin seems fair to us. *The Two believes their selflessness justifies their pride.* They keep a vault in their memory filled with every helpful deed, every act of generosity, and every instance of sacrificing their own preferences for the benefit of others. This mountain of evidence allows the Two to confuse their pride with humility.

Your Encounter with Jesus, the True Helper

As the Two encounters Jesus, they discover someone who empathizes with them—the True Helper. *As is true for the Two, Jesus' needs were ignored by others who always wanted more from him.* As much as Jesus focused on the needs of others, we see very few examples of people being concerned with Jesus' own needs. In the Gospels, lines formed and crowds gathered to be healed, fed, and taught. During Jesus' times of retreat and solitude, crowds would often hunt him down. The people who surrounded Jesus were far more concerned with what he could offer than what he might have needed. Many saw Jesus as a vending machine of miracles and free food, and they

LIKE THE TWO, JESUS' NEEDS WERE IGNORED BY OTHERS WHO CONSTANTLY WANTED MORE FROM HIM.

were thankful for the gift while ignoring the Giver. When the Two screams out, "When will these people appreciate me?" it's helpful to remember that Jesus understands what it's like to be taken for granted.

They also discover that Jesus models a better way of life for them. How does he display his authority? *Jesus affirms the True Self of the Two by serving others.* I don't think we fully appreciate the contrast between God's kingdom and Rome's kingdom. At the time of Jesus' ministry, Tiberius Caesar Augustus was the ruler of the Roman Empire. Tiberius would later be chronicled for his cruelty and exploitation of his servants. He gruesomely tortured his enemies for entertainment, and his sexual abuse was among the vilest in human history. He ruled millions of people and used them for his own pleasure and gain. In contrast, when declaring his agenda in ushering in God's kingdom, Jesus announced, "The Son of Man did not come to be served, but to serve" (Matthew 20:28). In first-century Rome, Jesus' rule was a *scandal.* Two kings with entirely different kingdoms. Whether feeding crowds, healing the sick or talking with outsiders, Jesus loved serving

LIKE THE TWO, JESUS SERVED OTHERS.

others and called his followers to do the same. The book of Acts tells us that Jesus taught, "It is more blessed to give than to receive" (20:35). Kings tell their subjects, "Lay down your lives for me." Jesus said, "I will lay down my life down for you."

Like the Two, Jesus befriended people. Well, not just people. He befriended strange people. He didn't seek out an exciting nightlife with the social elite or hobnob with the celebrities of his day. He didn't travel to Jerusalem to network with the power brokers. He chose friendship with people of low social status in the first century—women, ethnic minorities, the unclean, and even his Roman oppressors. He preferred the company of nobodies and outcasts. The Pharisees became so frustrated with his choice of friends that they finally exclaimed to his disciples, "Why does your teacher eat with tax collectors and sinners?" (Matthew 9:11). His closest friends—the disciples—were not among the respected class either.

They were described as "unschooled, ordinary men" (Acts 4:13) to whom Jesus declared, "I have called you friends" (John 15:15). Like the Two, Jesus brought outsiders in.

However, Jesus also confronts the False Self of the Two by allowing himself to be served. We are told that shortly before the Passover, Jesus was visiting the home of his friends Mary and Martha. After

JESUS CONFRONTS THE TWO BY ALLOWING OTHERS TO SERVE HIM.

dinner, Mary suddenly opened a bottle of expensive perfume and proceeded to pour it over Jesus' feet. She began to weep and wipe his feet with her hair. In many ancient cultures, a woman's hair was associated with her self-respect and her worth. Mary was not giving Jesus some small token of affection. She was showering Jesus with her prized possession, her raw emotions, and her social dignity. She was giving Jesus the gift of herself. He didn't shame her by refusing her gift. Jesus received this gift with gratitude and acceptance.

There is a story in the Bible about Jesus washing his disciples' feet (John 13:1–17). When I was a younger man, I decided to mimic this event by washing the feet of people in my small group at church. Among those present was my mentor. As I washed his feet, I felt a small taste of what Mary must have felt the night she poured her perfume over Jesus. It felt far more intimate than I had anticipated. I respected this man so much that I was moved to tears as I knelt before him, holding his bare skin in my hand. After I finished, he then took the bowl and towel from me and asked me to remove my socks and shoes. Instantly, I resisted. It felt wrong. I had so much respect for this man that his offer felt obscene. I was not worthy. Then I remembered that Peter had resisted Jesus in this similar situation. Jesus insisted that to know him, Peter must receive from him. I relented. It turns out that while giving love is vital, learning to receive love is too.

Jesus did not need to be indispensable. Ironically, Jesus was perhaps the only person in human history without a god complex. He came to save the world, and yet it's estimated that 80 percent of his ministry took place within a radius of twelve tiny square miles. Even among this small place, Jesus knew his limits and needs. Unlike so many Twos who run themselves into the ground, we see Jesus take a different trajectory as the demands grow. Pastor John Mark Comer writes, "In Luke's gospel in particular, you can chart Jesus' life along two axis points: the busier and more in demand and famous Jesus became, the *more* he withdrew to his quiet place to pray."[11] People who think they are indispensable don't withdraw to be alone. To top off his odd approach to ministry, Jesus left his disciples in charge and ascended to heaven. He gave them the tools they needed, and then he left. Hardly the decision making of an insecure or prideful person.

How did Jesus do all of this? How could he be so compassionate and befriending and yet never succumb to the allure of pride or indispensability? *Jesus trusted that the Father wanted him for who he was and not what he offered.* The gospel of John tells us, "The Father loves the Son and has placed everything in his hands" (3:35). In other words, the Father and Son have a deeply secure relationship. Jesus had no fear of being unworthy of love, no shame about who he was. Jesus knew that "the Father loves the Son." Jesus knew he was loved, and in this assurance he reached out to generously love others.

Redeeming Your True Self: From Manipulation to Unconditional Love

Jesus looks past the long line of the needy, the beggars, and the sick to see the inner world of the Two. He likes their befriending, compassionate character and their warm attention to the wounds

THE TWO IS GIVEN THE GOOD NEWS,
"I CHERISH YOU FOR WHO YOU ARE,
NOT WHAT YOU GIVE."

of others. As someone who also loves to be generous and serve people in need, he sees his own heart in theirs. He knows about their unmet needs, the neglect they've suffered in silence, and their deep fear that they're unworthy of love. He knows about their idol of being indispensable and their pride. To the Two, he says, *I cherish you for who you are, not what you give.* The Two finds in the gospel the very thing they've always wanted—to be worthy, treasured, and loved unconditionally.

The love of Jesus is not a wage to be earned. It's not some relational stock market that rises and falls according to our investments. We are told that nothing can separate us from the love of God (Romans 8:37–39). Brennan Manning writes, "His love is never, never, never based on our performance, never conditioned by our moods—of elation or depression. The furious love of God knows no shadow of alteration or change. It is reliable. And always tender."[12] In Jesus, the Two has now found the one who unconditionally cherishes them.

The Two has a wound of shame that whispers, "I'm not worth being taken care of." God says, "I am your Creator. You were in my care even before you were born." Jesus says to the Two, "I have not come just to be served by you, but to serve you." This is why Philippians 4:6 tells us, "In every situation . . . present your requests to God." God wants us to share our longings, desires, and hopes with him. He finds pleasure in giving us gifts. In Christ, the Two finds that God loves them for who they are, not what they do. God invites them to enjoy life *with* him and not merely a life *for* him.

Is it *possible* that God truly loves us with no strings attached? What if all the good things we do—our sacrifices and gifts and gestures—are incapable of shifting the scales of his roaring delight for us? What would happen if we let the mind-blowing reality of God's affection pierce the most hidden parts of our hearts? What could happen if we let the Holy Spirit tend to our wounds and convict us to turn from our sin? Our lives and our relationships would change.

First, we should probably take a moment to grieve. By genuinely regretting our past wrongs, we uncover the winds of transformation. We can't break free from the lies we believe without looking at the harm that believing those lies has caused. Pride has judged and demeaned others, left the Two unable to ask for help, and deformed their relationships by erasing personal boundaries. Eyes that look down on others cannot also look up to God. (If the Two really wants to give pride a kick in the shins, they can try confessing this sin to others and asking for forgiveness.)

Second, to counteract their pride, the Two will want to practice the virtue of *humility*. In many ways, humility and pride are fundamentally a battle between facts and falsehood.[13] True humility isn't competing to be the lowliest servant or make the biggest sacrifice. It isn't pretending to devalue ourselves or brush off compliments. As author Tom Holladay writes, "Humility is not denying my strengths; it is being openly honest about my weaknesses."[14] It's the ability to say, *Listen up, self! You need to come to grips with the fact that everyone doesn't need you all the time. And you need more sleep. But also, stop brushing off compliments by posing as an incompetent nincompoop when you're actually pretty great at a lot of things. You're not indispensable, and you're also not worthless.* Humility is simply the commitment to stay in reality. There is a God—and we aren't him.

TO COUNTERACT PRIDE, PRACTICE HUMILITY.

HAVE A REALISTIC VIEW OF YOURSELF THAT INCLUDES BOUNDARIES, NEEDS, AND ASKING FOR HELP.

Knowing they are cherished, the Two can stop using help-fulness as their identity. First Peter 5:5 reads, "All of you, clothe yourselves with humility toward one another, because 'God opposes the proud but shows favor to the humble.'" Humility allows the Two to steward their service in the way of Jesus. Humility allows us to admit we need help. Pride despises asking for help. Humility sets us free to open our hands to receive love.

A Two I know had recently developed hobbies and relational boundaries. She was even starting to take personal retreats and long naps. Noticing the difference, I asked her what had happened. She said she realized one day, "Wait. I'm just as important as all the people I help. I am worth taking care of." She even started calling me to ask for help when she needed it. This is humility in action.

When the Two practices humility, their life begins to grow a variety of good fruit. *First, humility allows the Two to practice and enjoy self-care.* One of the first signs of a Two becoming healthy is their ability to prioritize and tolerate solitude. Being alone allows the Two to get in touch with their own emotional needs and desires in life. Whether it's journaling, enjoying a hobby, getting more sleep, or exercising, humility allows the Two to be filled back up so they don't give beyond their limits. (Self-care is not selfish. Self-care is putting on your oxygen mask before you help anyone else.) One Two told me, "I had to learn to pay attention to myself—to my emotions and my body. Everyone kept telling me their ideas of what I should do to rest. I realized *I* had to figure out what was restful for me and what my own needs were."

Second, humility allows the Two to receive from others. In Matthew 10:8, Jesus said, "Freely you have received; freely give." To give to others freely, we first have to learn to receive from others freely. Receiving from others is the pathway to believing we are worthy of love.

Third, humility allows the Two to establish boundaries. They don't make knee-jerk decisions to fix everyone else's dilemmas. They understand there is a difference between being *concerned* about someone else and being *responsible* for someone else. When the rich young man disliked Jesus' teaching, he went away sad (Mark 10:17–22). Jesus did not chase him. He allowed the young man to go. Jesus practiced healthy boundaries, and now the healthy Two can as well.

Discipleship: Hospitality and Centered Prayer

To keep themselves from sliding back into the ditches of boundlessness and people pleasing, the Two will want to walk with Jesus through spiritual disciplines.[15] *To enhance their gift of service, the Two should practice hospitality.* By practicing hospitality, the Two can imitate Jesus—who loved sharing meals, sharing time, and befriending people in their time of need. Hospitality is about an open door, not a clean home. Whether through hosting dinners, serving in the community, assisting at church, or providing meals to the sick, the Two should seek to do this with no expectations of how others should respond. If we give with strings attached, we have hidden a hook inside our generosity. That's not love; that's deception. By practicing openhanded generosity, the Two can walk in the lifestyle of Jesus.

The other discipline is solitary prayer. This one will sting at first. It's a bit like dealing with an overtired toddler who had too much sugar, stayed up too late, and is now losing their ever-loving mind. Moving them from frenzied chaos to the stillness of sleep will not be granted easily. A boundless, people-pleasing Two who is addicted to the needs of others will not go gently into the night. Yet this is exactly what they need. Jesus invites them to come in solitary prayer to him. By sitting in silence away from people and devices, the Two is invited to notice and relinquish the urges to act, perform, and do. This approach may include repeating a meaningful word such as *worthy* or *delight*, or even simply sitting in silence. Solitary prayer is the means by which God breaks the alluring lie

THE TWO REFLECTS GOD'S
COMPASSION & CARE.

that the Two is only loved because of their actions. By sitting alone with God, they can receive his delight and commune with him.

If changing were easy, everyone would do it. We can expect our egos to fight us, our minds to recycle old thoughts, and our hopes to be dashed from time to time. However, as the Two walks with Jesus, they can learn to live less from their wounds and can be shaped more into the likeness of Christ. The False Self can fade and the True Self can shine. Transformation takes time and effort, but we can have better relationships with God, ourselves, and others.

As we have said, each of the types reflect a specific aspect of God. *The True Self of the Two reflects God's compassion and care.*[16] Philippians 2:7 says that Jesus has taken "the very nature of a servant." Paul reminds us "to do good, to be rich in good deeds, and to be generous and willing to share," so that we "may take hold of the life that is truly life" (1 Timothy 6:18–19). And of what value is this life to the world around us? Jesus says, "By this everyone will know that you are my disciples, if you love one another" (John 13:35). With their shame healed by receiving God's delight, the Two is now able to give the unconditional love they have longed for themselves. The compassion and generosity of the Two being experienced among the body of Christ is a living, breathing declaration to the world that the love of God is real!

Practical Tips for the Two

1. Check in with yourself daily. Before you begin your day, recognize your own feelings and thoughts and consider how they're shaping your life today.

2. Learn how to build boundaries. Learn to say no (or maybe) before saying yes. Read books about boundaries.[17]

3. Schedule intentional time alone. Give yourself some of the attentiveness, care, and pampering you usually give to others. Relax. Reflect. Pray.

4. Practice receiving without offering anything in return. Let gifts and acts of service be reminders that God and other people love you for who you are.

5. Lead people to solve their own problems instead of solving it for them. Learn to ask good questions that help people find self-clarity.

6. Write words of affirmation to yourself. Self-deprecation isn't humility. Humility is rehearsing the truth to ourselves.

CHAPTER 7

TYPE THREE
THE ACHIEVER

God loves your unedited self,
not your performance.

My friend Jenn has been driven her whole life. When you're with her, you feel a bit like you can do anything. She's like a motivational speech in the flesh. Jenn told me that as a kid, she learned that when she combined her natural gifts with hard work, doors of opportunity would open for her. She used this combination to push herself to get good grades, earn a college scholarship, and join influential clubs on her college campus. Her affable nature and the joy she experienced socializing resulted in a large network of friends.

After graduating from college, she suffered the setback of being turned down for a variety of jobs before finally landing an entry-level position with a large company in her hometown. Between her charm and her growing business skills, she moved up the corporate ladder, leading to a position where she negotiated business deals with Wall Street as well as successfully pioneered a European branch for the multibillion-dollar company she worked for. However, once standing at the top of the ladder, she realized it wasn't the life she wanted. In a bold move, she moved back to the States, resigned her position, and eventually took a job at a homeless shelter, where she oversaw their marketing and fundraising efforts.

This is how Jenn and I met—each working at separate shelters. To be honest, I was perplexed why a woman with her résumé was spending her life working with our city's poorest citizens. It turns out the answer was pretty simple: she loved Jesus and wanted to use her skills to help people in need. She had tasted the height of success and found it didn't live up to the hype.

Fast-forward several years. One day, I approached Jenn with an idea to launch a missions program for young adults. With so many nonprofits in our city short-staffed and so many young adults lacking professional skills, I wondered if we could find a solution for both of these problems. Maybe we could use this idea to build an opportunity to disciple young adults to follow Jesus and also to help people in poverty while we were at it.

Not only did Jenn encourage my vision, but she quickly signed up to serve as a founding board member. For almost a decade, Jenn has coached me and cheered me on as I fumbled my way through each stage of our organization's growth. Year after year, she has helped Love Thy Neighborhood tweak our goals, staffing needs, and support network. Jenn has coached me and inspired me to envision the type of person I want to become and the leader our organization needs me to be. (She also helped me envision writing this book.) If Yoda had become a life and business coach, he might have turned out something like Jenn.

If you have the drive, communication skills, and goal-oriented mindset that Jenn has, you may be a Three.

When the Three is healthy and living from their True Self, they're effective, driven, and goal-oriented. A Three with a clear vision and goals is like a master sailor at sea. The wind seems forever at their back, pushing them toward the future. They're at ease as they knock items off their to-do lists and fulfill their commitments. Whether targeting small things like getting their errands done before ten in the morning or big things like negotiating a profitable deal for their company, the forward-looking and energetic Three finds pleasure in achieving their objectives. These folks

don't usually require much babysitting. Because they have such a high value for competency, they're not only going to be self-starting, but they're also likely to be very good at whatever they start.

If you ask a Three to speak publicly in front of a group, they may hem and haw about it, but once the microphone is in their hands, it's as if the room fades to dark and a spotlight turns on. Whether they're with a friend over coffee, in front of a group on a stage, or speaking to the unknown masses on a podcast, the Three often reveals themselves to be a compelling communicator and storyteller. The healthy Three especially loves to use this gift to inspire, empower, and motivate others to take on new challenges and overcome obstacles. They are the most adaptable of any type on the Enneagram and can quickly adjust their communication style and posture to connect with their audience. They know how to "read a room" and have a sixth sense for knowing what motivates others.

As a member of the Heart Triad, the Three is highly relational and sees life as a web of interpersonal connections. The healthy Three not only perceives the emotional realities of those near them, but they honor their own inner worlds as well. The Three doesn't tend to *feel* their emotions so much as *do* their emotions.[1] The healthiest Threes have learned to slow down long enough to get in touch with the emotional world hiding behind their flurry of activity.

The Three makes a natural leader. They're good at networking, team building, and attracting the right people for a job. A healthy Three values people over projects and often creates a warm, humanizing environment. Instead of seeking out the limelight for themselves, many Threes actually prefer to coach others to chase their dreams as they cheer from the sidelines.

Many Threes are so goal-oriented they often achieve big goals early in life . . . and often find those goals weren't quite as satisfying as they anticipated. These Threes are less inclined to believe that happiness is found by climbing the ladder of worldly success. They resist getting sucked into social media popularity, beauty pageants, and the accolades of life in favor of following their own convictions. A healthy Three may not be as popular, but they're definitely happier.

Because the Three is so active and future-oriented, they experience a special connection to God whenever they sense he is doing something new. As new possibilities and pathways come into view, the Three becomes pregnant with visions of the future and begins searching for pathways to bring them into reality. The Three enjoys joining God and his people by launching new efforts to solve the problems of the world around them. However, the healthy Three does not allow their *doing* to replace their *being*. They enjoy the authenticity of transparent relationships with God and with other people in which they can lay aside their roles in life, let down their guard, and honor their emotions.

False Self

When the Three loses touch with the Spirit of God, they descend into a superficial expression of themselves. They overidentify with their need to succeed. They come to believe that what is *outside* of them matters infinitely more than what is *inside* of them. They find their value in what they produce and how others perceive them. Whether through their job, physical appearance, or income, the unhealthy Three broadcasts themselves as the ideal of success. They fixate on their image and how others view them. They become addicted to positive attention. One Three I know says he remembers the day

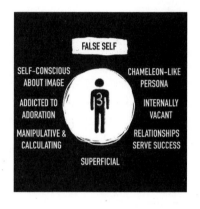

as a kid he realized he was funny and charming, "It was like I had just discovered I had superpowers. I could command an entire room of people with ease. I was in awe of what I was capable of."

Not every Three falls into this trap due to self-absorption; some fall into it due to misguided selflessness. One Three I know grew up in a world nurtured by violence. His mom did her best as a single woman to raise three sons. Yet both of his brothers ended up in prison, before one of them was murdered. This Three absorbed the responsibility of being the one son who would overcome their hardships. After graduating from high school, he moved to a new city and landed a well-paying job. He told me, "There's a lot of pressure on me to get out and make something of my life. No one gets out. I need to be different." If you look at the admiration this Three receives from his community back home and combine it with the pain his family has suffered, it's easy to see why he feels so driven to succeed. His success gives hope to his community and his failure could result in his mother losing another son to violence. He sees that his successes and his failures impact the lives of those who are depending on him. Knowing this makes the drive to protect his image of success more understandable. It also makes success powerfully seductive.

By being so externally focused, the inner world of the Three can often atrophy. Because they think other people only value them for their success, many Threes don't realize they can become shallow. They lack curiosity or concern for their own emotions (which often means they don't know what their true emotions even are). Similarly, because they believe that other people admire them primarily for their success, the Three can end up misrepresenting or embellishing themselves to edit out unflattering details. Truth becomes a matter of function, not a matter of reality.[2]

This inauthenticity makes their relationship with God challenging. The Christian faith can end up being worn like a fashionable outfit—something showcased to the public but taken off behind closed doors. As long as God *works*, he is useful. However, connecting with God at an emotional and vulnerable level can become downright confusing for the unhealthy Three. They only understand how to function *for* God, not how to be *with* God. Why confess their sins, admit their failures, or ugly cry in front of friends? That seems like an unnecessary mess when there's work to be done.

Childhood and Adolescence: Performance and Achievement

Most parents want their kids to get decent grades, be competent in a hobby they enjoy, and have some ambition in life. So for the Three, their childhood was shaped by the theme of *performance and achievement*. Many Threes share stories from their earlier years of participating in sports, dance, theater, or music (or *all* of them at the same time!). They learned early in life that combining their natural gifts with hard work can bring satisfying levels of success.

While many Threes knew they were loved unconditionally by those around them, they could still sense a special pride from their family or friends when they succeeded. There's no way around the fact that getting tenth place will get you a hug and some encouraging words, but getting

THE CHILDHOOD THEME OF THE THREE IS PERFORMANCE & ACHIEVEMENT.

first place will get you a parent who looks like the Beatles just arrived in America for the first time.

The young Three found that their own sense of value rose and fell according to the adoration of the people around them. As teens, when their clothes and body shape were desirable, they drew people in. When they weren't, they pushed people away. When they achieved second place or made mistakes during a performance, they felt embarrassed and could sense that others were not as impressed with them. This small insecurity would grow over time into something much crueler.

With so much emphasis on performance and achievement, the Three interpreted an unspoken message: *It's not okay to have your own feelings and identity.*[3] As a child, the Three found that what they felt, what they were curious about, and what may have been stirring inside them was of little consequence or importance. Being admired paid off more than being authentic. One Three told me, "I used to tell my sister to just play the game. Just do what they ask, and you'll get their approval. It doesn't have to be authentic or what you actually want." To a kid who doesn't know the difference, approval and love seem like the same thing.

Like all people do, at some point the Three asked themselves, *Who am I?* Between the sports, the grades, the stages, and the performances, a voice inside replied, *You're as valuable as your last achievement.* As a result, the Three became *afraid of being worthless or without inherent value.*[4] This became the fuel that drove them to succeed. The Three came to believe that if they are not successful, beautiful, or admired, it will confirm their deepest fear: their life is a smoke screen to hide the pitiful truth that they are a worthless loser.

Take a kid who is scared they're worthless, who senses that everyone's adoration rises and falls according to their performance, and who sees failure as a threat to being accepted, and you've got a kid who feels a lot of *shame.*[5] The Three learns that to attract people, they must be attractive. To get and keep love, it helps to put on a good show.

Behind their clubs, sororities, job titles, certifications, and business ventures is just a kid longing to be esteemed, to have someone value them and tell them, *"You are loved for yourself, not your performance."*[6] They want to know what love feels like when they no longer have to impress anyone.

THE THREE WANTS TO BE
VALUABLE.

Like all of us, the Three *wants to be valuable.*[7] Without a stable sense of value, we feel insecure. We want to know we're safe from abandonment and can rest in the security of our relationships. We want to be able to share our ideas and experiences and have someone else say, "Wow! That's a huge help. Thank you for sharing!" We want to know that our qualities and character are beneficial to others. The Three isn't looking to be important to *everyone*; they just want to be important to *someone.*

Unfortunately, somewhere inside their hearts, this good desire to be valuable gets corrupted. They overshoot their target, and as a result, their journey can take an unintended, darker path.

Nurturing Your False Self: Mistaking Success for Value

When I was growing up, my divorced parents fought like Republicans and Democrats. If one said gravity made things fall, the other one would find a way to take offense and launch an assault. After every battle, they'd each retreat to the closest televisions they could find so they could forget about the drama that had just unfolded (as well as fail to notice that both of their kids were hiding in their rooms). The simple task of dropping off my sister and me at the other parent's house was a traumatic event. We'd pull into the driveway and rush to get inside the house as fast as possible. The last place we wanted to be was out in the front yard where our parents might interact and start a war. Their proximity to one another was gasoline and matches. They were combustible, and we were wearing flannel.

However, there was one place where they always called a truce—public events where their kids were on stage. As my sister and I would stand on stage getting an award or singing a song or eating fire in a circus (another story for another time), we would look out and see Congress joining a bipartisan effort to cheer us on. As a kid, I was both baffled and intoxicated. At some deep level, my sister and I got the message that our parents were happiest when their kids were succeeding. I don't think even heroin is as addictive as the feeling of making your parents happy. They may not have known how to attend to our emotions, but our parents sure knew how to clap, smile, and make eye contact when their kids were wowing the world in front of an audience.

This is the drug that gets injected into the heart of a young Three. They want to be valuable, but *they settle for the idol of being successful.* Why? They can't tell the difference between personal value and personal success. The looks of admiration they receive when they achieve

AUTHENTICITY W/ THEMSELVES & OTHERS

FAMILY & INTIMATE RELATIONSHIPS

BEING LOVED FOR WHO THEY ARE

THE IDOL OF THE THREE: BEING SUCCESSFUL

feel like love, and the looks of disappointment they see when they fail feel like shame. Growing up, they asked themselves the question, *Who am I?* and they now have an answer: *I am successful.*

The idol of being successful requires sacrifices. The Three sacrifices intimate relationships, authenticity with themselves and others, and being loved for who they are and not what they do.

What happens when the Three puts their hope and identity in being successful? They grow the deadly sin of *deceit*.[8] The burden of always having to succeed is heavy. It's an unsustainable business plan. In order to feel valuable, the Three believes they must succeed

HOW DOES THE THREE NURTURE THEIR DEADLY SIN?

SPINNING STORIES

AVOIDING CONFESSION

DECEIT

CURATED PUBLIC IMAGE

ENDS JUSTIFY MEANS

100 percent of the time or—at the minimum—maintain an *image* of success. Whether or not that image represents the truth is irrelevant, as long as it results in being valued and loved by other people. They curate themselves for maximum adoration. The ends justify the means.

To maintain that image, sometimes a little editing is required. Like using photo filters on our phones, the Three learns to enhance, trim, and adjust who they are and how they portray themselves to others. They simply edit out the zits, the bulge, and the dirty laundry of their life experiences. The problem with filters is that they're not enhancements; they're lies. They don't represent who we truly are.[9] One Three shared about his relationships: "Am I a chameleon, or do they like the real me? Do *I* even know the real me?"

Before they lie to anyone else, they first lie to themselves. Self-deceit is an ever-present threat. They put on a mask and think the reflection they're seeing is their own. James Cofield of CrossPoint Ministry once told me, "They're selling their Kool-Aid, but they're drinking it too."

To cope with the pressure to perform and maintain their self-image of being successful, the Three defends themselves through *identification*[10]—a defense mechanism where a person identifies more with the successful "role" they are playing than with their own authentic self. Identification is a way of bolstering one's self-esteem by forming an imaginary or real alliance with an admired person and then taking on that person's characteristics. When the Three models their own behavior after someone else, or the idea they have of someone else, they are usually not aware they are doing so.

If this stuff came out in the real world, it would sound something like, "Have I casually *name-dropped* the people I know, the leaders I've worked with, the awards I've won, the associations I've been invited to join, or the deals I've landed? No? Let me go ahead and do that now. Impressed yet?" And, of course, we usually are.

Maybe the young Three's dad showed his approval by covering the walls at home with trophies and awards. Maybe Mom was typically a little aloof but suddenly gave undivided attention on game day. Maybe the boys in high school all wanted to date them because of their good looks. Or maybe the girls told them how much they respected their ambition. Regardless of how it happened, they learned to stuff away their own feelings and desires to get admiration from the people they needed it from. We can't fault a kid for becoming dependent on the thing that gave them the value they longed for. But we also can't let that kid continue to believe the lie that people only deserve to be valued when they're successful. Dogs and ponies have to put on a show to prove their value; people don't.

In the context of our life experiences, each type's deadly sin makes sense and feels natural. *The Three believes their success justifies their deceit.* They see some lies as helpful, as necessary, and even as good. Crafting a persona and looking successful bring adoration from others. Because adoration feels like delight (the remedy for shame), deceit feels necessary to the Three. Their image is a shield to protect them from humiliation.

So, the Three finds themselves in a quandary. If they stop succeeding or stop appearing successful, they risk becoming worthless. If they keep deceiving themselves and others, they're living in a fantasy and lighting a match to any hope of genuine relational connection. They want someone to see them as valuable but don't know how to find it without showing off their impressive résumé.

Your Encounter with Jesus, the True Achiever

As the Three encounters Jesus, they find someone who understands their pain. *Like the Three, Jesus failed to fulfill the crowd's demands to be a successful leader.* It seems that

at every turn Jesus proved to be a disappointing Messiah. The people of Israel had visions of a mighty war hero who would come and overthrow the tyranny of the oppressive Roman Empire. We're told on one occasion that after Jesus performed many miracles, a group of Jews attempted to "make him king by force" (John 6:15). Later, the same crowd that applauded him as he rode into Jerusalem would shout for his crucifixion. Jesus was mocked for being such a messianic failure by having a robe and a crown of thorns placed on him and the mocking title "King of the Jews" inscribed above him on the cross as he died. Jesus understands what it means to disappoint people's expectations and lose their admiration.

However, Jesus also displays his authority and mastery of life. *First, Jesus affirms the True Self of the Three by being visionary.* His vision was singular: inaugurate God's kingdom and make citizens of that new kingdom. He taught his disciples to pray to the Father, "Your will be done, on earth as it is in heaven" (Matthew 6:10). He baptized the

LIKE THE THREE,
JESUS FAILED TO FULFILL THE CROWD'S
DEMANDS TO BE A SUCCESSFUL LEADER.

imaginations of his disciples with a vision so profound and deeply rooted that they devoted their lives (and, in most cases, *sacrificed* their lives) to bring that vision into reality. As Richard Rohr says, "He could reach the masses, and in every situation he found the right words to bring his message to the people. He could hold discussions with scholars and move the hearts of the simple, uneducated country people."[11] To encounter Jesus was to encounter a world that is and is to come.

LIKE THE THREE, JESUS WAS VISIONARY.

Like the Three, Jesus also affirmed having goals. Jesus lived a focused life. Goals help us understand what our next steps should be and what we should prioritize. Consider all the goals we see Jesus pursue—to memorize the Scriptures, to recruit disciples, to heal the sick, to practice silence and solitude, to travel town to town, to proclaim the good news, to commune with God, to befriend the outcast, to fulfill his calling from the Father. He also made it clear that his followers are expected to bear fruit (love for neighbors, self-sacrifice, intentionality, and so forth; see John 15:8). Jesus was ambitious, and his life proved it.

However, Jesus also confronts the False Self of the Three through a bad reputation and a lowly status in the eyes of people around him. While other rabbis had a highly selective process for choosing their students, Jesus basically did the equivalent of walking up to strangers in a Walmart and asking them if they wanted to join him on a road trip. His approach wasn't

JESUS CONFRONTS THE THREE BY CHOOSING TRUTH OVER ADMIRATION.

exactly reputable. It seemed like everyone with fame, popularity, or power disliked him. Every time Jesus amassed large audiences, he seemed to sabotage the type of success his listeners wanted from him by saying something offensive. He was horribly inefficient as he traveled—constantly stopping to interact with individuals instead of pushing onward to get to the crowds. Unlike the unhealthy Three who is drawn to the spotlight, Jesus seemed to avoid traveling to powerful cities, making influential friends, or lounging in luxury.

Jesus chose truth over being admired. Jesus had the communication skills, leadership, and charisma to have been accepted by the religious leaders and celebrated by the masses. Instead, he kept talking about love, grace, and justice, which cost him the acclaim that was within his reach. Standing in front of a crowd and saying something you know they're going to be angry about has to be just about one of the bravest things anyone can do. That kind of maneuver is social suicide. If only Jesus would have had a PR team. They could have at least advised him on how to soften his language, "Listen, I was reviewing your sermon—it's great by the way—and I think calling people blind and telling them there will be . . . how did you phrase it? . . . 'weeping and gnashing of teeth,' well, it's not a good look. What are some kinder words we could explore instead?" But Jesus was wise enough to proclaim, "Woe to you when everyone speaks well of you, for that is how their ancestors treated the false prophets" (Luke 6:26). Popularity and righteousness are not synonyms.

How could Jesus avoid yielding to the deadly sin of deceit? Why didn't Jesus become a workaholic addicted to admiration? *Jesus trusted that his Father loved him for himself, not for his work.* The love of the Father was so acute and ever-present that Jesus wanted all of his followers to experience the same intimate, authentic, transparent love (John 17:23). Jesus never mistook his mission as the reason the Father loved him. Jesus did not need the admiration of others, because he knew he was loved, regardless of his reputation.

Redeeming Your True Self: From Image to Authenticity

Good news for the Three: Jesus finds pleasure in who they are. As someone who is also visionary, energetic, and inspirational, he appreciates them. God knows the shame that the Three carries, their fear of being worthless, and their deadly sin of deceit. He sees that they feel enormous pressure to put on their best face, to wow others,

THE THREE IS GIVEN THE GOOD NEWS.
"I LOVE YOUR UNEDITED SELF,
NOT YOUR PERFORMANCE."

and to prove their value. God sees all of their efforts to appear successful. Jesus says to them in the stillness of their heart, *"I love your unedited self, not your performance."* The Three finds in the gospel the very thing they long for—to be inherently valuable and worthy of love.

Their impressive social network, career achievements, and charm that usually hypnotize people doesn't work on Jesus. He's not impressed. They could blunder their big sales pitch, accidentally tuck their shirt into their underwear for everyone to see, have a booger hanging out of their nose all day, and get called to the mat for exaggerating their success stories—and do you know what would happen? The look of love and adoration in his eyes wouldn't soften. They could land a book deal, launch a network, make seven figures a year, or have their product sold in every Target in the world—and do you know how he'd react? He'd be happy for them, but he still wouldn't be impressed. For Jesus, our value has nothing to do with our success or our failure. Jesus wants to enjoy our company and hear our voice, no matter what. In Jesus, we're immune from auditioning. First Samuel 16:7 tells us, "The LORD does not look at the things people look at. People look at the outward appearance, but the LORD looks at the heart."

Indeed, Jesus himself was not impressive in his outward appearance. Isaiah tells us, "He had no beauty or majesty to attract us to him, nothing in his appearance that we should desire him" (53:2). The Three might be beautiful or successful or powerful, but none of that has any impact on their value. In childhood, the Three believed they had to perform to receive love and affirmation. In Christ, the Three finds they are delighted in, just as they are—no parades, fashion shows, or magic tricks required.

What might happen if the Three decides they believe that God loves them for who they truly are and not for their performance?

First, they can grieve. We live in an era where we tell people they shouldn't ever feel guilt or remorse, which is utter silliness. Grief can work like smelling salts to wake us from our slumber. Our lives have been diminished and harmed by deceit. It's kept us from being honest, prevented us from bonding deeply with others, and driven us to say or do things that are against our convictions. If we refuse to take an honest inventory of the damage we've done, we cannot repair our relationships. Confessing our sin of deceit to God and others and asking for forgiveness is the pathway to restoration. Grief is not the destination, but it's an important stop on the journey to a new life.

Second, to counteract their deceit, the Three will want to *practice the virtue of truthfulness.*[12] Real love requires people, not actors. A public persona may get us social media likes, but it'll never make us happy. The exhausting work of performance may attract people to us, but it will never make them stay. If we're selling people on

our features, they'll only hang around until an upgrade becomes available somewhere else. Here's what makes a person stay: we show up as our authentic selves and learn how to give and receive love.

Nothing is more valuable than authentic intimacy. Unfortunately, nothing is scarier either. Whatever the soul's equivalent of flabby arms, double chins, and love handles is, Jesus is asking us to bare it all. The Scriptures tell us that David was a man after God's own heart (1 Samuel 13:14; Acts 13:22). For years, I thought this description was referring to David's performance and achievements. But then I actually read the Bible. David was a disaster. Murdering people, assaulting a woman, disobeying God, asking for mercy for his own sins but destruction for others because of their sins.

Why was David's heart like God's? I think it was because he was authentic and open. He was genuine and wanted genuine connection: "The LORD is near to all who call on him, to all who call on him in truth" (Psalm 145:18). I much prefer the first half of the verse. The first half feels like ordering a pizza; the second half feels like shark cage diving. The risk of authenticity feels dangerous. And yet there is no other way to be near to God—we must be willing to show up authentic and open.

One Three told me, "Sometimes I used to put myself around people who were good for my career but bad for me personally. They made misogynistic or even racist comments, but they helped my career. Sometimes I didn't say anything, or I'd even nod my head because I didn't want to rock the boat. But I'm done with that. I speak up more now. I am trying to lean into who God has made me. At the end of the day, who cares if I lose those people? They aren't healthy people for me anyway."

Being truthful allows the Three to reveal their desires, dreams, conflicts, and insecurities with transparency. Honesty renounces spinning stories, doing sales pitches, name-dropping, and walking the runway in favor of true relational intimacy. Intimacy is where we experience love, acceptance, and value. It allows us to get real about who we are. One Three told me, "I decided I don't like gyms, so I stopped going. I decided I like cardigans, so I bought some. I kept trying to learn to play golf so I could network with business leaders. I didn't enjoy it, so I stopped playing. I decided to stop doing things simply because I needed others to like me and started to learn what I like for myself."

When the Three practices truthfulness, their life begins to grow a variety of good fruit. *First, the redeemed Three becomes reliably present to their loved ones.* Whereas the Three was often distracted by their own goals and work, they learn to slow down and attune to the emotional and relational needs of those around them. This often looks like turning off cell phones, striking up a good conversation, and losing track of time with the people we love. It's learning to relate by *being* together and not just *doing* together.

Second, they develop authenticity. They must find a small group of people with whom they can share their unedited self. In other words, this group of friends needs access to the Three's inner, intimate life—successes *and* failures, celebrations *and* confessions. Through experiencing openness, acceptance, and affection from this group of friends, the Three can come to believe that God also loves them unconditionally. Then the Three can say, along with the apostle John, "So we know and rely on the love God has for us" (1 John 4:16).

Third, they develop a better work-life balance. The drug of workaholism will lose its power. The Three will keep boundaries around their work and protect their time away from their job. They'll practice resting and Sabbath. In time, the margin that has been achieved will allow them to see God at work around them in ways they had previously been too busy to notice.

Discipleship: Study and Confession

To keep themselves from falling back into the trap of workaholism and deceit, the Three will want to practice two spiritual disciplines.[13] *The first discipline the Three will want to practice is active study*—a discipline that will probably feel pretty natural. This practice may include doing Bible studies, following reading plans, taking theology courses, or joining reading groups. It is the acquisition, exploration, and expression of knowledge about God. Many Threes find group studies or a 365-day Bible reading plan especially helpful, since it gels with their goal-oriented instincts. To live in truth we must first know the truth.

Second, the Three will want to practice the spiritual discipline of confession. This particular spiritual discipline is a direct assault on the vanity and persona of the Three. When we confess our sins, we're kicking the legs out from under the lie that tells us, "If anyone ever knew the truth, they'd hate me." Unconfessed sin makes us sick from the inside, scared that everyone around us has X-ray vision and knows the truth that we're a glutton or a pervert or a liar. We're terrified that if we confess the ugly truth, we will end up all alone. But confession works like a key that lets us out of solitary confinement. When we confess our sin with appropriate specificity to trustworthy friends, a spouse, or a pastor, we often catch glimpses of God's unconditional love and healing power at work (James 5:16).

The Three is notorious for wanting to set the land speed record for personal transformation. Unfortunately, our False Self rarely coordinates with our timetable. It intends to keep using its same old effective tricks to lull us back into our trance. We should anticipate that it will take time, grace, and grit to change as people. And yet

THE THREE REFLECTS GOD'S
VISION & FRUITFULNESS.

Jesus promises that lies won't have the last word. John Mark Comer writes, "Ideas have power only when we believe them. We hear all sorts of ideas every day, some brilliant, others ridiculous; but they have zero effect on us unless we begin to trust them as an accurate map to reality."[14] If we're saying that Jesus defines what is real, then we must also decide that it is a lie that we're only as valuable as our successes. If Jesus defines reality, then Jesus defines our value.

Each of the traits of the Enneagram—when healthy—reflect a different aspect of God's character. *The True Self of the Three reflects God's vision and fruitfulness.*[15] In believing that God loves them for themselves and in living truthfully with God and other people, the gifts of the Three can be restored. The Three can truly reflect the efficiency of God to the world. Before the fall of humanity in the Garden of Eden, God established work as good. To create the world, God worked. To share the gospel, Jesus worked. Even now, the Holy Spirit continues to work inside each of us. The gift of the Three reflects God's productivity and fruit to the world. Colossians 3:23 reads, "Whatever you do, work at it with all your heart, as working for the Lord, not for human masters." We work as an act of worship, not to prove our worth.

Practical Tips for the Three

1. **Find a couple trusted friends to be vulnerable with.** Try scheduling a consistent time each week at a private place to share with each other.

2. Redefine success. How would Jesus define success? What would happen if you adopted his definition?

3. Live outside the spotlight. Enjoy your life off the stage exploring hobbies that are unrelated to your work.

4. Value your feelings. Check in with them daily and be honest about what you feel. Emotions are critical for discernment and wisdom.

5. Confess your failures out loud. Everyone fails. We'll never believe God's grace is real until we confess to others and they love us in response.

6. Separate from your image. Likely, the public "you" and the private "you" are different. What would happen if you nurtured the private "you" more?

CHAPTER 8

TYPE FOUR
THE ORIGINALIST

*God delights in you because you're
you, not because you're different.*

M any years ago, one of my dear friends, Aaron, was shooting a documentary film in Alaska about the dangers of the crab fishing industry when his vessel capsized. Most of the crew was swept away into the cold dark of the sea, including Aaron. He was never seen again.

He was a founding member of our little church, and his death devastated our community. In the middle of worship services, people would break down crying and wailing. In the months that followed, we turned to the Scriptures and found countless passages that echoed our grief and pain. However, when we turned to the contemporary worship music of our time, we struggled to find songs that helped us lament. Most of the music on Christian radio had very little to offer a community being swallowed up by sorrow. We needed songs for broken hearts.

A group of musicians from our church gathered over several months to express their grief through music. They ended up writing and recording an album that opens with the lines, "All I feel is broken and weary to the bone. I've given up the fight and found I have no strength to carry on. Let me run to you. Draw me close and hold me tight. Be the strength that I don't have and in my weakness shine."[1] These musicians brought us emotional honesty and words for our grief through beautiful music. They gave us the gift of lament.

If you're authentic, emotionally deep, and drawn to beauty like these folks, you might be a Four.

True Self

At their best, the Four uses their gifts to bring depth, empathy, and healthy self-expression into the world. As a member of the Heart Triad, the Four is emotionally sensitive and empathetic, and they excel at giving language to the emotional experiences of life. Typically uninterested in surface experiences, they are natural deep divers searching for treasures buried in the fathoms of the human heart. Because they are not scared of deeper existential terrain, one of their gifts is being near to those who are mourning and grieving. They aren't scared of dark emotions, dark questions, or dark truths and can help others feel permission to wrestle with these hard realities.

With a love of beauty (in people, places, and things), the Four often prefers things that are unique, interesting, or handcrafted. They tend to be aesthetically gifted and artistic. They express their creativity through unique fashion, home furnishings, and hobbies.

The Four also has the ability to see the ordinary world as

miraculous and profound. They often see the mundane as baptized by the presence of God. Like the psalmist, their worship and prayer life is emotionally expressive, transparent, and raw. They are sensitive to God's prompting to take action—especially in advocating for justice for the oppressed. The Four experiences a unique connection to God when they create. They join God in his creative work by bringing texture, color, and vibrancy into the world.

False Self

When the Four is unhealthy, they overidentify with being different. They become dramatic and moody. I once had a Four tell me that during her senior year of high school, she was sitting at lunch when a freshly printed yearbook was handed to her. Inside, she discovered that she had been voted "Most Dramatic" by her classmates.

Feeling humiliated and enraged, she stepped up onto the table in the school cafeteria, faced her perpetrators, and screamed at the top of her lungs. She then walked outside and set her yearbook on fire as the whole school watched through the windows in stunned confusion. Now in her early thirties, she laughed as she remarked, "I might have been a bit overreactive."

Their general disposition can be summarized as *differentiation*. They *have* to be different. One Four confessed to me, "If I'm honest, I often say I dislike something only because other people like it, not because I've actually given any true thought to it." I know another Four who often grimaced and refused to laugh when watching comedies with her friends, only to go watch the movies again in secret, where she openly laughed. In private, there was no need to be different from others.

The unhealthy Four tends to fixate on what is missing and habitually feel misunderstood. They want whatever they *cannot* have and don't want what they *do* have. They feel that something is missing and become anxious to find themselves somehow deprived of the mysterious contentment others seem to have. This can lead to developing an emotional bond with their fantasies instead of with real people.

Of course, they relate not only with other people through this lens but also with God. Just as they see themselves on the outside of their social groups, they view themselves outside the attention of the Father. They feel shame and self-pity for being overlooked by God and hold him accountable to their standards of goodness— finding him cruel for not fulfilling their longings. In times of worship, they find songs of lament comforting and authentic while disdaining songs of joy and celebration. They feel ashamed of who they are and cannot entertain with any seriousness the reality of God's adoring love for them.

Childhood and Adolescence: Loss and Rejection

At some level, everyone deals with abandonment as a child. But for the Four, when they look back on their younger years, *loss and rejection* is a theme tattooed on their heart. This theme can show up in a million different ways— emotionally distant parents, being given up for adoption, the death of a loved one, or just the general feeling that they are card-carrying members of the Island of Misfit Toys. It doesn't really

WHY WAS I ABANDONED?

THE CHILDHOOD THEME OF THE FOUR IS LOSS AND REJECTION.

matter whether their interpretations match historical events or are just their imagined perceptions because the impact is the same: the Four carries a haunting notion that they've lost their sense of being connected to others and can't seem to get it back.

Somewhere deep inside, the Four has a suspicious belief that they caused their own abandonment. The idea that our parents, our aunts and uncles, our teachers, or our neighbors were sometimes horrible people is nearly impossible for a kid to believe. What hope is there if all the adults are broken? It's a lot easier to swallow the pill that we cause our own problems. Even though they were just a child who had no control over the actions of adults or other people, they subconsciously believe, *People don't abandon valuable things but I was abandoned, so that must mean something is wrong with me.* If you understand that this is one of the earliest building blocks in the psyche of a Four, it makes it a lot easier to understand why they sometimes cry harder than everyone else.

This theme of loss and rejection leads the Four to the conclusion that *it's not okay to be too different or too alike.*[2] They think that perhaps they were abandoned for being too much (too weird, too needy, too emotional, too expressive), but they're also convinced that if they just simmer down and restrain their too-muchness that they'll be forgotten, overlooked, and inauthentic. They end up in a game of neurotic seesaw, constantly trying to decide whether to go full throttle with their self-expression or to dial it back so they don't freak people out. It feels like a battle between life in a cubicle and life in a Salvador Dali painting.

Determined to be dissimilar, unhealthy Fours can be eccentric, snobby, and contrarian. Their self-expression turns into self-indulgence, where they create self-fulfilling prophecies of rejection by behaving in ways that ensure they will be misunderstood. Oscillating between inappropriately oversharing and stubbornly withholding, in social settings they can become anxious, wondering what others think of them. Retreating in shame, they can become withdrawn and introspective to the point of being cynical, dark, and troubled. Convinced their own deficiencies are the root of the problem, they can become self-hating. They have a compulsion to locate their pain and express it to others—a backward way of trying to gain sympathy and avoid abandonment.

All of this wrestling over self-expression and social rejection leaves the Four feeling insecure about their identity. They ask the question, "Who am I?" Why? The Four *is afraid of not having a distinct identity or personal significance.*[3] When God was creating humanity, for the Four, it's as if everyone else made all the stops on the assembly line in an orderly fashion to be assigned their identity, but somehow they ended up with the word *defective* stamped on their foreheads. The Four is afraid that their identity is incomplete—that others possess special qualities they do not. They become haunted by a search for the missing pieces they can't seem to find.

If you take a kid and pump them full of feelings of loss, rejection, insignificance, and a premature identity crisis, you end up with someone who is experiencing a lot of *shame.*[4] The Four believes their flaws make them unworthy of being loved, accepted, and cherished. They're embarrassed and self-conscious about who they are. They feel stuck in a dream where they accidentally went to school naked. Any moment, all the kids are going to notice that their classmate is uncovered, and the looks of pity and sounds of laughter will erupt.

Inside their big, expressive heart is just a kid who wants someone to understand them, celebrate them, and tell them, *"I know you and delight in you for who you are."*[5] Delight only comes when we give our focused attention to something. We lose track of time as feelings of pleasure and joy wash over us because of our revelry in the thing we are paying attention to. The Four longs to be someone's best-kept secret—receiving adoring special attention from someone who loves them.

This is why the Four tends to put a lot of stock into finding a person who can deliver this message to them. Find an adoring boyfriend or girlfriend. Marry an adoring spouse. Give birth to an adoring child. Surely one of these people will deliver this message in a believable way. However, fantasy and reality rarely align, and eventually people do disappoint. Unable to ever find what will fulfill them, the Four comes to love the thrill of the chase, not the catch. In fact, the Four can become sad and quickly lose interest when they finally catch their object of desire. Unsatisfied and on the hunt once again, this longing makes it difficult to be present in the moment. The Four easily gets lost in a romanticized memory or an idealized fantasy. The bigger the gap between their fantasized relationships and their real relationships, the more disappointment they feel.

THE FOUR WANTS TO BE THEIR AUTHENTIC SELF WHO IS SIGNIFICANT TO OTHERS.

At their core, *the Four wants to be their authentic self who is significant to others.*[6] This is the good and decent thing that every human wants—the freedom to be their genuine selves and to be loved for who they are.

However, somewhere deep in their personality, this emphasis on being their authentic self gets supercharged and twisted.

Nurturing Your False Self: Mistaking Being Different with Being Authentic

I once paid good money for a silver ring that turned out to be a fake. What I thought was authentic turned out to be a counterfeit. The Four makes this same critical mistake in their subconscious. Instead of turning to God, and because they can't find someone who will love them as their authentic self, the Four *settles for the false idol of being different.* Why? Because they can't tell the difference between being

HAPPINESS

FEELING ACCEPTED & UNDERSTOOD

EVERYTHING COMMON

THE IDOL OF THE ORIGINALIST: BEING DIFFERENT

authentic and being different. For them, these two characteristics seem identical. Being different becomes a fixation. It begins to shape their imagination, their social life, and their view of themselves. It promises to make them special, unforgettable, and one-of-a-kind. They grew up haunted by the existential question, "Who am I?" and they now have an answer: "I am different."

However, the idol of being different requires sacrifices. They must sacrifice being happy, enjoying "common" or "popular" things, and feeling accepted and understood. Being different hates the idea of being understood. It's hard to be dark and mysterious when all the lights are on.

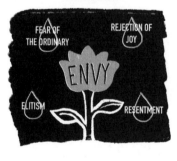

HOW DOES THE FOUR NURTURE THEIR DEADLY SIN?

FEAR OF THE ORDINARY

REJECTION OF JOY

ENVY

ELITISM

RESENTMENT

What happens when the Four puts their hope and identity in being different? They grow the deadly sin of *envy*.[7] They focus on what they lack through comparing themselves to others. That other person has more friends, makes more riveting art, makes more interesting conversation, has more unusual clothes, has the perfect romantic partner, and so forth. When we're envious, our insecurities trap us in a loop of comparison. We see ourselves *in contrast* to other people. We become sad about the happiness of others and happy about the sadness of others.

Heaven forbid that a Four should come across someone who seems relationally happy, secure in their identity, comfortable in their body, and competent in their achievements. Envy will have no rest. The very presence of a secure person feels like a firing squad on our soul. Their beauty only reminds us of how ugly we are. Dorothy Sayers writes, "Envy is the great leveler: if it cannot level things up, it will level them down . . . Rather than have anyone happier than itself, it will see us all miserable together."[8]

To cope with loss and rejection and maintain their self-image of being different, the Four defends themselves through *introjection*[9]—a counterintuitive defense mechanism where a person absorbs negative information (and repels positive data) about themselves as a way of protecting against threats. "Oh? You think you understand me? No you don't." "You said you liked ninety-nine things about me, but you said one bad thing. I know which one is true." "You love me? What about that time three years ago when you were so mean to me?"

The Four suffered as a child. Life was often dark and relationships were painful. The Four takes into their psyche a lost person, characteristic, or event and deeply identifies with its loss. Maybe Dad was a neglectful narcissist or Mom was a TV-binging recluse. Maybe Brother was mentally ill or Sister moved as far away as possible to find freedom. Or maybe home was a refuge from the bullies and the "perfect" families who can't stop giving the eccentric Four the side-eye. So the Four now walks with a limp. The problem is that the limp is now part of their swagger. Instead of going through the process of grieving and eventually healing, and then moving forward into life, the Four holds on to their pain and sadness as central to their identity. But grief is supposed to be a process, not a home.

What really makes our deadly sin dangerous is that it feels comforting and reasonable. *The Four believes their pain justifies their envy.* All the memories of being rejected, abandoned, misunderstood, and overlooked make envy seem like the most natural and decent response to getting shortchanged by life. This allows the Four to confuse their envy with righteous discontentment.

Your Encounter with Jesus, the True Originalist

One of the first things that the Four should take note of when they meet Jesus is that he empathizes with them. *Like the Four, Jesus was rejected by his community and constantly misunderstood.* Some seven hundred years before Jesus' birth, the prophet Isaiah told us about the Messiah who was to come: "He was despised and rejected by men, a man of sorrows and acquainted with grief; and as one from whom men hide their faces he was despised, and we esteemed him not" (Isaiah 53:3 ESV). "Man of Sorrows" was a well-suited title.

JESUS, THE TRUE ORIGINALIST

SENSITIVE

CREATIVE

AVOIDS
SELF-PITY

ORIGINAL

LOVES
BEAUTY

OFTEN
MISUNDERSTOOD

COMFORTABLE BEING BOTH
DIFFERENT AND ORDINARY

Jesus' entire life was influenced by loss and rejection. His mother's pregnancy was gossip fodder for a small town. His birth was marked by a threatened king who killed infant boys. When Jesus was twelve, his parents misunderstood his intentions and scolded him. In adulthood, his hometown, the religious leadership, and the Jewish crowds all rejected him. His friends misunderstood him constantly. One of his friends eventually betrayed him, resulting in Jesus' torture and execution. At every turn, the very people he was trying to love responded with skepticism, confusion, or rejection.[10] It's as though Jesus were saying to the Four, "You may tell other people they don't understand you, but you don't get to say that to me."

LIKE THE FOUR,
JESUS WAS REJECTED BY HIS COMMUNITY
AND CONSTANTLY MISUNDERSTOOD.

The Four also sees Jesus display his authority and mastery of life. *Jesus affirms the True Self of the Four by valuing emotional expression—including lament.* When Jesus arrives at the burial site of his friend Lazarus, he finds Mary and Martha distraught with grief at the loss of their brother. They are confused by Jesus' absence when they needed him. Mary does what a lot of us in our grief do—she blames God. Whereas I tend to scream at the heavens and tell God to stop sleeping on the job, Mary says it more factually: "Lord, if you had been here, my brother would not have died" (John 11:32). Jesus doesn't get offended and say, "Oh? You think you know better? Let's switch places and see how you do as God." Instead, he weeps. He already knows he will raise his friend

LIKE THE FOUR, JESUS VALUED EMOTIONS, INCLUDING LAMENT.

and be reunited with him in mere moments, but instead the Man of Sorrows takes time to shed tears with his friends at the pain of loss. God grieves.

Like a Four, Jesus also expressed originality. What a hard guy to predict. In one moment he answers his accusers with stinging wit and the next he says nothing at all. In one instance he heals a man with mere words, and in the next he heals a guy using mud. He broke all the archetypes. He was assertive *and* gentle, bold *and* meek, compassionate *and* firm, faithful to the Scriptures *and* capable of offering new insights. He broke social mores, built a core team of commoners, and seemed to prefer the company of people who would have been kicked out of Christian universities or rejected by churches. He affirmed the dignity of women in a society where their testimony wasn't even admissible in court. He was a disturber of the peace who confronted both corrupt institutional sin and individual sin. And yet he spoke of God's grace and love in ways no one had ever heard before. He was impossible to predict and unlike any other person—a true one-of-a-kind.

However, Jesus also confronts the False Self of the Four by avoiding the need to be different. One of the primary reasons he was rejected as the Messiah by so many was because he was such a common man. They had expected the Messiah to come in power and grandeur. Instead, he looked like most of his peers. He grew up in a small rural town, learned the family trade, and was so poor that he often relied on the generosity of others to survive. The Messiah was supposed to be dressed in splendor, not hand-me-downs. When he began to reveal timeless secrets and truths about God, the world just shrugged its shoulders: "Isn't this the carpenter's son?" (Matthew 13:55). He confronts the Four's need to be different by choosing common people to be his disciples. These are blue-collar men without much education. Being special or unique or having elite cultural taste are not prerequisites to being valued by Jesus.

Jesus also called his followers sheep. If you ever want to pick a

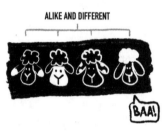

ALIKE AND DIFFERENT

JESUS CONFRONTS THE FOUR
BY CALLING THEM SHEEP.

fight with a Four, call them a follower. The Four looks at mainstream culture and thinks to themselves, *Look at all those pitiful sheep.* Yet Jesus says that the Four who follows him is one of the sheep too. He strikes at the ego and elite standards of the Four. He describes himself as the good shepherd who loves his sheep and leaves behind everything to find them. In this way, Jesus tells the Four, "You are not as different from everyone else as you think you are." One Four told me the most freeing thing a counselor ever told her was, "There's nothing special about you."

How was Jesus sensitive and creative without ever succumbing to the deadly sin of envy? Why didn't Jesus feel that he *needed* to be different? *Jesus trusted that his Father knew him and delighted in who he was.* Jesus was known and celebrated by his Father (Matthew 11:27). Yes, other people misunderstood him, but his Father didn't. Other people were reluctant to accept him, but his Father always accepted him. Unlike us, who get ravaged by crippling insecurity hiding behind grandiose egos, Jesus always had a secure sense of identity because he knew who his Abba was.

Redeeming Your True Self: From Dreaming to Action

Good news for the Four: Jesus has a special affection for outcasts, misfits, and weirdos. They're his people. He likes their originality, their depth, and their emotional honesty. He likes their quirkiness and their intensity. After all, he shares these same qualities. He knows about their unmet longings to be seen and loved, their idol of being different, and their envy. To the Four he says, *"I know you and delight in who you are."* The Four finds in the gospel the thing they ultimately want—to be themselves, known, and celebrated.

THE FOUR IS GIVEN THE GOOD NEWS.
"I KNOW YOU AND DELIGHT IN WHO YOU ARE."

The Four frequently believes their emotional depths are unknowable by others. However, the psalmist reminds us that this is not true:

> You have searched me, LORD,
>   and you know me.
> You know when I sit and when I rise;
>   you perceive my thoughts from afar.
> You discern my going out and my lying down;
>   you are familiar with all my ways.
> Before a word is on my tongue
>   you, LORD, know it completely.

You hem me in behind and before,

and you lay your hand upon me.

Such knowledge is too wonderful for me,

too lofty for me to attain" (Psalm 139:1–6).

We may be a mystery to ourselves and others, but we're not a mystery to God. We are known.

In Christ, the Four finds that God loves them for who they are. The Four says to themselves, *If I was valuable, I wouldn't have been abandoned. However, I was abandoned, so I'm worthless.* Jesus responds, "Look at the birds . . . Are you not much more valuable than they?" (Matthew 6:26). In Christ, the Four is no longer abandoned. The lost has been found.

At times, life has been hard and sad for the Four. Jesus doesn't tell them, "Always look on the bright side of life." He invites them to grieve—to get unstuck. We are reminded that "the LORD is close to the brokenhearted" (Psalm 34:18). By going through the process of grief, the Four is healed and can begin to experience joy (Isaiah 61:3). In turn, the Four can respond with the affirmation of Psalm 30:11: "You have turned my wailing into dancing; you removed my sackcloth and clothed me with joy." God won't let sorrow have the final word.

So let's just say the Four decides they believe that God sees them and delights in them. Let's just say they let the Holy Spirit work some of this healing and joy down into their bones. How can they respond? They can follow Jesus as yet another one of his ragtag disciples trying to live a new way of life. They can awaken from their trance that has convinced them of a thousand lies and live in the truth that Brennan Manning expresses so beautifully: "Define yourself radically as one beloved by God. This is the true self. Every other identity is illusion."[11]

First, it would help to *admit to ourselves that our envy has hurt our relationships and to feel some grief about it.* Envy has been the fuel for discontentment, insecurity, and resentment. Envy has prohibited gratitude and kept us from noticing or celebrating God's goodness at work in and around us. It has made us hostile to others, socially anxious, and likely pretty depressed. We can't justify our envy and also walk in the way of Jesus. It's hard to love people and be envious of them at the same time. Remorse helps us realize, "I don't ever want to act that way again," and can be motivation to do the hard work of change. Admitting our envy to others and making amends are pretty good steps as well.

Second, to counteract their envy and emotional reactivity, the Four will want to *practice the virtue of emotional equanimity.*[12] Equanimity is not the pursuit of disowning or denying emotions; it is the response to the specific experiences of life with exactly as much feeling and energy as is appropriate and necessary without exaggeration. It means we discipline ourselves to not freak out every time something triggers us emotionally. Equanimity allows the Four to honor every emotion without the compulsion to express every emotion. It makes emotions into a team player. Emotions can be in the car, but they aren't allowed to put wisdom and obedience in the trunk.

TO COUNTERACT ENVY,
PRACTICE EMOTIONAL EQUANIMITY.

RESPOND WITH EXACTLY AS MUCH FEELING AND ENERGY
AS IS APPROPRIATE AND NECESSARY WITHOUT
EXAGGERATION.

Jesus practiced equanimity when he prayed, "Give us today our daily bread" (Matthew 6:11). He believed that God the Father would give him exactly what he needed moment by moment and day by day. Jesus practiced equanimity when he wept, but he also practiced it when he restrained his anger during his arrest. Jesus neither overreacted nor underreacted. He did not manipulate through moodiness or through detachment. Jesus did not nurse wounds. Equanimity allows the Four to steward their emotions in the way of Jesus.

When the Four practices equanimity, their life begins to grow a variety of good fruit. *First, equanimity allows the Four to develop gratitude and satisfaction.* Instead of fueling their envy by exclusively focusing on the gap between their dreams and their real-world experience, the Four learns to celebrate. They express gratitude and delight and see the happiness and flourishing of others as evidence of God's abundant love, not as a threat to their own fulfillment. I know one Four who makes a habit of encouraging the people she meets with handwritten notes, small pieces of art, and words of affirmation. After interacting with her, people always leave feeling built up and celebrated.

Second, they develop a sense of belonging. Equanimity allows the Four to recognize a handful of people in their life who care deeply about them. Though these friendships are flawed, they can also still be good. The Four often feels they have been left out of friendships and life events. However, through Jesus, they can now see that they are a part of the family of God—the body of Christ. Instead of waiting on the sidelines to be noticed, they are able to proactively pursue and participate in relationships and shared life experiences. They are not outsiders but equal members of the body of Christ, where there is both relational unity and individual diversity.

Third, they begin to take action. Instead of depending on their ever-changing moods to give them clarity on what they should do, they begin to develop discipline and routines that decide the rhythms of daily life. They get organized by creating structure and supportive habits to live an active lifestyle designed to cultivate goodness.[13] They move past their daydreams, fantasies, and over-thinking and begin to act on their ideals.

I know one Four who says that equanimity allowed her to move past her fantasies into reality. She came to serve as an urban mission-ary with Love Thy Neighborhood. She told me, "Actually working with the poor really killed the romance of mission work. It showed me reality and forced me to decide: Am I going to keep fantasizing about helping people in need, or am I going to take action and *actually* help people? I decided to stop chasing my emotions and do something for others instead. That experience changed my life."

Discipleship: Silence, Solitude, and Feasting

To keep from falling back into their old way of viewing life, the Four will want to walk with Jesus through two spiritual disciplines.[14] *The natural discipline for the Four to practice on a regular basis is silence and solitude.* Turn off phones, power down laptops, close the door, and go into isolation for a bit. Tell everyone that unless they want the Moody Monster to terrorize the house that evening, you need some alone time. Use this time to daydream, to imagine, to pay attention to your inner world, and to journal. Also, especially turn your attention to the lives of others through prayer—try to remember your aunt's cancer, your coworker's marriage problems, and your pastor's needs.

The other discipline is feasting. This is a time to gather with others for the purpose of celebration. Scheduling regular times of feasting with friends will help the Four escape from their navel-gazing and focus on other people. It will directly combat their melancholy and their tendency to become pessimistic by filling their senses with good food, good friends, and good laughter. It's a perfect way to remember the goodness of God that is still at work in the world. It's a movement from sadness to laughter, from wailing to dancing, from sitting alone in our bedroom listening to sad music to drinking in the vibrancy of God's good gifts together. To feast is to practice gratitude and joy.

By no means should we naively believe that God will instantaneously heal our wounds just because we believe the gospel. Old habits never die easily. However, as the Four walks with Jesus, they can live less from their wounds and more from their hope. The False

Self can diminish and the True Self can grow. As Romans 12:12 says, "Be joyful in hope, patient in affliction, faithful in prayer."

The True Self of the Four reflects God's depth and creativity.[15] Fours are able to see that the ordinary world is actually quite extraordinary. What others may take for granted, the Four is able to see as

THE FOUR REFLECTS GOD'S
DEPTH & CREATIVITY.

remarkable evidence of God's good work (Psalm 104:24). In addition, they are incredibly adept at adding emotional language to life—thereby helping others more wholeheartedly understand the experience they're living. With their shame healed by God's delight, the Four can bring their gift of creativity and emotional depth to God and others as a gift. The aim of their work becomes to form life-giving connections with God and others, not as a means of gaining attention to heal their wounds. In Christ, their wounds are already being healed. The Four invites us all to be our authentic selves who live in the freedom of Christ!

Practical Tips for the Four

1. Catch yourself excessively fantasizing. This is a flashing light, warning you that danger is ahead! You are on a fast track to discontentment!

2. Recognize when your wounds are speaking. If you're wanting to hide, overexpress, or manipulate, it's not the Holy Spirit prompting you.

3. Practice celebration and gratitude. Out loud. Written down. In your mind. Do it as a disciple of Jesus, not dictated by your emotional waves.

4. Respond instead of react. Consider that maybe *you're* the one

who misunderstands. Guard against your impulse to create drama and intensity.

5. Create structure and supportive habits to live an active lifestyle. God made you to dream, but he also made you to *do*. Action makes dreams reality.

6. Don't withdraw when you're hurt or overwhelmed. Self-Sabotaging 101. It's a surefire way to feel abandoned. Take a breather and reengage.

THE HEAD TRIAD
Searching for Security

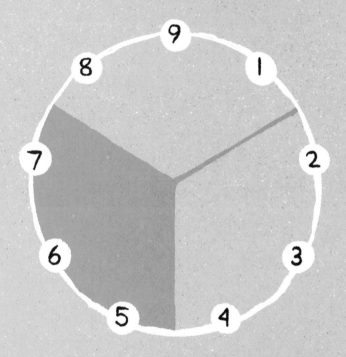

CHAPTER 9

TYPE FIVE
THE INVESTIGATOR

*Your needs are met by God's care, not
by understanding everything.*

A friend of mine held a movie premiere for his latest film about break dancing and gang life in Guatemala. The event included a break-dancing competition. Hundreds of people filled the old warehouse to watch. After a little liquor, the event quickly became rambunctious. I've never cared for the taste of liquor, but let me say this: drunk break dancing is quite a sight to behold.

At one point during the evening, I looked over to see my friend Jim. Jim's characteristics are polar opposites of the evening's characteristics. Whereas the event was loud, crowded, and rowdy, Jim is soft-spoken, spacious, and tranquil. He's got a real Obi-Wan Kenobi meets Captain Spock kind of vibe. When you're with him, you just feel wiser.

Throughout the night, I watched Jim slowly walk around the warehouse and carry on a series of one-on-one conversations with our friends. Eventually, he made his way to me, where he asked about my family and probed my thoughts about some of the themes of the movie. He listened patiently as I fumbled through some disorganized thoughts. When I asked him the same question, he spoke philosophically about the soul's need for community. Soon he made his way to the host of the event, where he gave a hug, offered compliments, and then slipped to the edges of the room.

Afterward, a dozen of us went to a nearby restaurant for a nice dinner. Jim sat and listened to the rest of us banter as we shouted unnecessarily loudly down the long table at one another. A few times, he turned to engage in quiet conversation with the person next to him, where he inquired about places they had traveled and recent books they'd been reading. As the dessert arrived, Jim and his wife said their energy was spent. After saying goodbye, they got up and left. A few minutes later, when we inquired about the bill, the waiter told us that Jim had already paid for everyone.

All night long, Jim asked good questions as he made quiet, reflective, informed conversation with those around him. Then he did a silent act of generosity without any fanfare and slipped away to recharge. If you're like Jim and enjoy being informed, thinking before speaking and getting energy through spending time alone, you might be a Five.

True Self

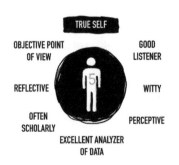

When healthy, the Five is thoughtful and reflective. As a member of the Head Triad, they process the world through their minds, which makes them highly curious and focused thinkers. The Five is gifted with synthesizing large amounts of data and complicated facts into something easy to understand for those around them.

To support their sharp analytical skills, the Five tends to speak less than any other type, especially in group settings. They prefer to gather data from observation and then organize their thoughts before sharing aloud. When they do finally share, their comments are often perceptive, objective, and wise. I once asked a Five if he knew he had a reputation for being wise. He told me, "Half the time I don't know what's going on. I just sit silently so I don't sound like an idiot. People just think I'm wise because I keep my mouth shut until I have something to say." Now, that's wisdom!

Naturally scholarly, they are highly intelligent and creative thinkers. They find tremendous pleasure in doing deep dives into things that trigger their curiosity, which allows them to be unusually insightful in their areas of expertise. Many Fives enjoy books, articles, philosophy, and documentaries. While the Five enjoys intellectually stimulating conversations with others about subjects that interest them, they frequently despise small talk. A Five once told me, "Do you want to know what hell is for a Five? It's having to mingle at a party for all of eternity."

The Five is perhaps the wittiest of all the types as well. Few things are funnier than a Five in a group setting as they make wry, incisive jokes delivered with perfect timing. It's usually a onetime, quiet performance, so if you ever have the chance to sit next to a Five at a staff meeting, I strongly encourage it.

The healthy Five brings their curiosity to God as well. They plumb the depths of the Scriptures and the riches of the Christian tradition. They seek clarity with God and abide with him in stillness and listening. Their ability to bask in silence and solitude allows them to achieve a deep knowing from God that surpasses data and facts. They allow information to support their relationship with God without mistaking the information itself as the relationship.[1]

False Self

When they're unhealthy, the Five overidentifies with their need to perceive. They move beyond objectivity and become relationally detached. Instead of merely backing up to see the whole picture, they just leave the picture altogether. They're prone to isolate and can become reclusive. Even if they don't retreat to their study, garage, or project, they may be physically present but relationally absent. In doing so, they become unresponsive and uncaring to the needs of others. I once visited an art gallery with a sign that read, "Make Suggestions and Requests Here." Upon filling out the card and sliding it through the small slot on the table, the sound and vibrations of a paper shredder could be heard and felt. This is how others can feel when dealing with an unhealthy Five.

Of all the types, the Five is the most aware of their resources. They are acutely aware of the finite limits of their energy, their time, and their money. Because of this hyperawareness of resources, they begin to see needs—especially emotional needs—as threats that will deplete them. As one Five sat with my wife and me, wrestling with her feelings about a guy she had become romantically interested in, she began to cry. Finally, she yelled, "This is so dumb! What a waste of my energy!"

Some Fives can fail to mirror other people emotionally in their facial expressions, causing those around them to feel ashamed. They don't mean to, but they can end up acting a bit like robots. They're so invested in their thoughts that they simply stop emoting. They'll have a conversation with you, but they've got a poker face that leaves you with no clue what cards they're holding. They could be falling in love with you or may just be thinking about making a sandwich. Visually, it's hard to tell the difference.

Believing the outer world will deplete their resources, the unhealthy Five will often withhold and hoard. They can have an "every man for himself" approach to life. Because they're so smart and informed, they can become arrogant and condescending. Of course, this arrogance is just a mask to hide their fear that they don't know enough.

This detachment brings profound harm to their relationship with God. God is transformed from being a loving Father to a set of theological concepts and ideas. Logic, facts, and study replace active relational engagement. In the same way that reading a book about skiing is not the same as actually experiencing the thrill and sensations of skiing, studying about God is not the same thing as knowing God himself. In many cases, even God is seen as too demanding for the finite resources of the Five, making him unrealistic to follow. This makes the journey away from a lived faith much easier. They withdraw not only from others but from God as well.

Childhood and Adolescence: Engulfed or Neglected

While everyone feels overwhelmed by life from time to time, *being engulfed or neglected* hangs over the Five's childhood years like a theme. Even as a kid, the Five saw the gap between the vast complexity of life and their personal resources. Many Fives report feeling overwhelmed by the world around them as kids.

THE CHILDHOOD THEME OF THE FIVE IS BEING ENGULFED OR NEGLECTED.

In some cases, this may have been a domineering parent who engulfed them, a passive parent who neglected them, or simply a community in which children were expected to find solutions to their own problems.

One Five shared that when she was a child, her parents divorced and arranged for shared custody. She suddenly found herself transporting an overnight bag and her favorite toys back and forth between houses multiple times a week. One day, she realized that neither adult in her life was able to stay aware of her day-to-day needs and that she would need to look out for herself. Another Five shared that he learned early in life not to bring his problems to his overreactive mother, who would blow the topic out of proportion. When he turned to his dad, he found a man who would underreact by listening but never actually do anything to help. As a result, he became reluctant to bring any issues to either of his parents. These are heavy burdens for a child to bear. No matter how it showed up, the message got through: "You're on your own kid. Hope you have a plan. There's a storm coming."

It's easy to see why these experiences lead the Five to subconsciously conclude that *it's not okay to be comfortable in the world.*[2] They came to believe that they could not assume others were going to take care of them or that there would be enough resources to survive. They started hunting for everything they needed to take care of themselves. Their minds became like fallout shelters, stocked to the brim with the information they would need in order to survive.

When we see the world as a resource-sucking, scarce wasteland trying to drain us of life, we can't help but see other people as just another mouth to feed with our limited supplies. The best thing to do is hunker down, take care of ourselves, and survive as long as we can. To do this, we must become survivalists who are capable, competent, and protected. Imagine Tom Hanks in *Cast Away* with a dash of an old man yelling, "Get off my lawn!" and you're in the ballpark.

This is why the Five is *afraid of being incapable, incompetent, or intruded upon.*[3] They have an existential dread that life will swallow them whole if they aren't ready. This can come out in big ways and small ways. Take a simple task like getting the oil changed in your car. This could easily turn into a three-week crisis for a Five, who isn't sure whether they should learn to do it themselves to save money or take it to the shop where someone will surely try to swindle them. It can show up in bigger areas too—especially their relationships.

As the Five attempts to survive life in a scarce world, the prospect of being close to others becomes especially difficult. If they can't master the measurable facts of skills and objects, how are they supposed to be competent in the immeasurable world of relationships? People are erratic and needy and let their emotions cloud their judgment. To be in a relationship is to remain a novice. As soon as you figure a person out, they change again and you have to start over. The Five feels pressure to be a Swiss Army knife—possessing all the capabilities and competency necessary to survive what may come, but they never have all the tools they need.

As a result, the Five has the underlying emotions of *fear and anxiety*.[4] When the Five is forced into a situation where they have not prepared or internally organized themselves, they cannot perceive a safe way forward. They are scared that both their own needs and the needs of others will overwhelm their resources and leave them stranded and depleted. A lot of people don't realize the Five is anxious because they're usually so calm and collected. But that's usually because the Five has redirected their energy away from their bodies and into their brains, where there's a lab filled with tiny NASA engineers scurrying around trying to figure out all of life's problems.

This fear leaves the Five believing that every need is just another problem to be solved. This is why so many Fives are minimalists. If you don't possess something, you aren't responsible for taking care of it. This works fine enough with pets and power tools, but it's a horrible approach to relationships—including our relationship with ourselves.

Of course, if we see our needs as a problem, the best thing to do is to not have any needs. If we can make our worlds small enough, our responsibilities light enough, our interactions with others minimal enough, we might just survive life on planet Earth. This is why the Five longs to hear the message, *"Your needs are not a problem."*[5] Imagine being stuck in a dust bowl—all of your crops long dead, dirt blocking out the sun as far as you can see—and someone shows up and says, "Actually, we've got too much food. We'd love to feed you and your family for as long as you need." The Five wishes they could believe there were enough resources in the world (and inside *themselves*) to care for their relationships, their finances, their vocation, their home maintenance, and so forth and so on. They

THE FIVE WANTS TO BE COMPETENT.

wish they didn't feel so much pressure to figure everything out on their own. They wish they didn't have to be scared to come out of their cave.

What drives the Five? At their core they just want to be *competent*.[6] They want to have the necessary skills and knowledge to live successfully. Who can blame them? None of us want to feel incompetent and unable to complete

our tasks. The world needs more people with wisdom, informed insight, and skills. These are good and godly desires, because being incompetent, uninformed, and thoughtless is a recipe for disaster.

The problem is that somewhere inside the Five the desire to be competent mutated into something insidious.

Nurturing Your False Self: Mistaking Knowing Everything for Competency

Instead of turning to God and trusting that he is the only one who needs to be all-knowing, the Five develops their own plan to enhance their competency. Since they can't be competent enough to cure their anxiety, *they settle for the idol of knowing everything.* They can't tell the difference between knowing everything and being competent. They mistakenly believe that being competent requires them to be intellectually omniscient. They have asked themselves, *Where am I?* and they now have a map to lead them forward: *As long as I know everything, I can navigate life.*

WHAT IS THE FIVE WILLING TO SACRIFICE?

FEELING KNOWN & LOVED | INTIMATE RELATIONSHIPS | ENGAGING LIFE

THE IDOL OF THE INVESTIGATOR: KNOWING EVERYTHING

However, the idol of knowing everything requires heavy sacrifices. They must sacrifice having intimate relationships, feeling known and loved, and being engaged in life. Life becomes a one-dimensional experience centered around the mind. They wrongly conclude that they understand cooking because they watched a documentary about it as opposed to actually preparing a feast with their own hands.

What happens when the Five puts their hope into knowing everything? They grow the deadly sin of *greed*[7]—especially relational greed. Simply put, they are so committed to being self-sufficient that they become selfish with their resources. If you're like me, you probably think to yourself, *I'm not greedy! I'm just being economical/prudent/levelheaded!* But as Tim Keller says, "Jesus warns people far more often about greed than about sex, yet almost no one thinks they are guilty of it. Therefore we should all begin with the working hypothesis that 'this could easily be a problem for

HOW DOES THE FIVE NURTURE THEIR DEADLY SIN?

HOARDS & WITHHOLDS | AFRAID OF NOT BEING ENOUGH

GREED

ENOUGH IS NEVER ENOUGH | WITHDRAWS FROM RELATIONSHIPS

me.' If greed hides itself so deeply, no one should be confident that it's not a problem for them."[8]

Ironically, the Five wants to thrive in life, but they're marked by discontentment. Because they attempt to thrive through greed, their inner life suffers. Proverbs 11:24 (ESV) teaches us, "One gives freely, yet grows all the richer; another withholds what he should give, and only suffers want."[9]

To cope with feeling engulfed and neglected, the Five defends themselves through *isolation*[10]—a defense mechanism whereby a person withdraws mentally, physically, emotionally, or relationally to avoid feeling overwhelmed and emptied. Because they feel overwhelmed, they isolate. Because they isolate, they feel lonely. Because they feel lonely, they're overwhelmed. It's a vicious cycle.

The loneliest moment for any person is when their mind is blown and they have no one to share their revelation with.[11] What benefit is pondering the mystery that there are more stars in the universe than grains of sand on earth if we are all alone? What good is knowing everything if we don't have anyone to share our discoveries with? However, this loneliness reveals the truth. As Richard Plass and James Cofield write, "What does loneliness tell us about ourselves? Be it chronic or acute, slight or significant, loneliness is proof of our relational design."[12]

The Five has felt overwhelmed and underresourced for most of their life. They're scared that they don't have what it takes to be competent at living. Maybe the Five had needs, and the people they needed to show up for them simply didn't. Maybe Dad disappeared and Mom was doing her best to just keep the bank from taking the house. Maybe home was an emotionally cold place that valued skills and independence over hugs and affection. No matter how it happened, the message came through that the Five had to find their own way in a world of scarcity. They're scared to rest because if they do, they'll either be inept or be taken advantage of when challenges arise. This fear has been significant enough that they are scared of their own emotions, scared to need other people, and scared of being swallowed by life. Their pain and anxiety are real. We can't tell a kid to figure it out on their own and then act confused when they grow up to be an adult who sees the world as a scary place that wants to eat them alive. Kids aren't meant to be scavengers.

Why is greed a *deadly* sin for the Five? Because they mistake it as necessary for life. Greed is reframed: *The harsh and unrelenting demands of life justify my greed.* Other people may end up left out in the cold without their bare necessities, but the Five will not. They believe each person needs to take care of themselves, which often requires some self-preservation in the form of withholding.

This leaves them feeling anxious, being greedy, and isolating from others. Is this what it means to be wise? What is the alternative?

Your Encounter with Jesus, the True Investigator

How does Jesus empathize with the Five? *Like the Five, Jesus was engulfed by the demands of a world that wanted everything from him.* The Scriptures record 113 questions that people asked Jesus. Crowds often swelled just as Jesus was attempting to withdraw to be alone and rest (Matthew 14:13–14). People often saw Jesus as a blessing to enjoy while avoiding the "burden" of actually knowing him (Luke 17:12–19). Jesus often spoke, only to have his words fall on unresponsive and

neglectful ears (Mark 6:1–6). The world had no concern for Jesus' own needs. If there is one thing humanity has always been good at, it's using God to get what we want. In the Gospels, we can see that enough was never enough for the crowds. They would always be wanting more. Jesus understands the pain of the Five.

LIKE THE FIVE,
JESUS WAS BOMBARDED BY THE WORLD
THAT WANTED EVERYTHING FROM HIM.

The Five also sees Jesus display his authority and mastery of life. *Jesus affirms the True Self of the Five by knowing the truth and being informed.* In the Sermon on the Mount (Matthew 5–7), Jesus dropped massive amounts of wisdom on everything from anxiety to sexuality, from how to handle enemies to how to build a meaningful life. Throughout his teaching, he references specific Old Testament passages (only possible by diligent study and intellectual effort) and then challenges the most common interpretations of those passages with brand-new insights. He pulls from history and theological analysis while remaining astute about the culture he was speaking to. The Scriptures tell us that "when Jesus had finished saying these things, the crowds were amazed at his teaching, because he taught as one who had authority, and not as their teachers of the law" (Matthew 7:28–29). Jesus was a well-informed, well-read man who was wise at all times in all situations. To discover Jesus is to discover wisdom incarnate.

Like a Five, Jesus was reflective. Luke 5:15–16 tells us, "Yet the news about him spread all the more, so that crowds of people came to hear him and to be healed of their sicknesses. But Jesus often

LIKE THE FIVE, JESUS WAS REFLECTIVE.

withdrew to lonely places and prayed." Unlike so many others who allow their schedules to overwhelm them to the point that they avoid slowing down, Jesus had a reputation for enjoying solitude. Richard Foster once wrote, "Our Adversary majors in three things: noise, hurry, and crowds."[13] Jesus knew this and led a direct assault on the devil's efforts. The more demanding his life became, the more he withdrew to pray. Even in his conversations with others, Jesus was reflective. He often asked them clarifying questions and repeated back words they had shared—both of which are signs of reflective listening. In our modern times, we've choked out wisdom with the weeds of hurry, chatter, and distraction. Jesus always made space to nurture wisdom.

However, Jesus also confronts the False Self of the Five by believing the world is full of abundance. In a competitive world with limited resources, needs are a net loss. No wonder some of us hide in our bedrooms, numbing ourselves behind the glow of a virtual world on our screens. In a universe of scarcity, tyranny, and neglect, we have no choice but to isolate and stockade our rations. Jesus was not like this. He did not mistake *accumulation* for *life*, and he confronts this lie directly. He reminds his disciples that God cares for the birds and so they have no need

JESUS CONFRONTS THE FIVE BY SEEING THE WORLD IS FULL OF ABUNDANCE.

to anxiously hoard: "Are you not much more valuable than they?" (Matthew 6:26). He tells his followers, "Whoever wants to save their life will lose it, but whoever loses their life for me will find it. What good will it be for someone to gain the whole world, yet forfeit their soul?" (Matthew 16:25–26). Jesus believed that life was abundant (John 10:10). There is enough for everyone.

Also, Jesus was not a loner. Though he often withdrew to lonely or isolated places, Jesus could hardly be called antisocial. His solitude often seemed to prepare him for engagement with those around him. Likewise, Jesus did not mistake discourse for relational intimacy. (A Five can sometimes oscillate between private study and public lecture and effectively skip relational intimacy altogether. But intimacy is the linchpin. Life doesn't work without it.) Jesus' life was marked by sharing meals, traveling with friends, and participating in the lives of those around him. Jesus understood that the gospel could never be understood if it were reduced to mere theological study. The gospel that people experience is the gospel they will know. Love cannot be understood by reading; love can only be understood by experiencing it—and that experience will always be in relationships.

How did Jesus live with such wisdom and objectivity without succumbing to the deadly sin of greed? Why wasn't he compelled to unearth every answer to every problem? *Jesus trusted that God was present with him and that his needs were not a problem.* Jesus said, "The one who sent me is with me; he has not left me alone" (John 8:29; see also 10:30; 14:9). Jesus knew in his bones that the Father was ever-present, never slumbering, always sustaining, forever tending. He knew his Father was aware of all of his needs and that he could trust God to care for him. The only thing that would ever overwhelm and engulf him would be the love of God.

Redeeming Your True Self: From Withholding to Acts of Love

THE FIVE IS GIVEN THE GOOD NEWS, "YOUR NEEDS ARE NOT A PROBLEM."

Jesus likes the Five. He appreciates their search for truth, their dedication to wisdom, their commitment to be slow to speak and quick to listen. He appreciates their need to recharge by being alone in solitude. I imagine if he were here, he'd enjoy a long, nerdy, in-depth exploration about the wonders of God's world. Jesus understands the Five. He knows about their unmet need to feel competent, about their idol of knowing everything, and about their greed. To the Five he says, *"Your needs are not a problem to me."* The Five finds in the gospel the very thing they want—to be competently capable of engaging life.

To know everything is not a burden meant for humanity. Since the dawn of social media, the number of people reporting high levels of anxiety has skyrocketed. One of the key reasons for this is that we simply aren't built to have God-sized amounts of real-time knowledge of the world. We simply can't master every angle on every issue. Anxiety is a sign of distress, revealing that we are not built to handle the load we are attempting to carry. If we can't carry this burden, who will? If we don't have all the answers, who does?

The antidote for the fear and anxiety of the Five is *the abundant presence of God.* Theologians use the term *omniscient* to describe God. He is all-knowing. Nothing escapes his sight. No problems arise that stump him. This is good news for all of us. If God doesn't know everything, then I must conclude that I have to. Of course, if God does know everything but he is a selfish jerk, that wouldn't help us either. If I can't trust that God knows what I need and loves me enough to provide it at the right time, my brain has no choice but to concoct survival plans. But Jesus offers a different option: "Come to me, all you who are weary and burdened, and I will give you rest. Take my yoke upon you and learn from me, for I am gentle and humble in heart, and you will find rest for your souls. For my yoke is easy and my burden is light" (Matthew 11:28–30).

Jesus' great desire is to respond to and meet the needs of the Five. The Five believes they must be frugal and withholding in order to take care of themselves, but Philippians 4:19 tells us, "My God will meet all your needs according to the riches of his glory in Christ Jesus." Jesus *wants* to care for you and meet your needs.[14] The Five believes the world will take everything from them and abandon them to their poverty. Jesus will do no such thing. This is why the author of Hebrews tells us, "Keep your lives free from the love of money and be content with what you have, because God has said, 'Never will I leave you; never will I forsake you'" (13:5).

So for a moment let's suppose that the Five is able to believe that God does not see their needs as a problem. Let's assume that the Five can consider that God is all-knowing and always present with them and has made them competent enough to engage life. The generous, attentive, omniscient presence of God is actively meeting their needs. How can the Five respond?

First, the Five will want to *consider the real damage that greed has done* to their life. How has greed pushed people away? How has it left others neglected? How has hoarding time, isolating, and ignoring relationships hurt people? Greed keeps us from seeing the abundance of God. It makes us fixate on the gap between where we are and where we think we need to be. Greed makes us *addicted to more.*

TO COUNTERACT GREED,
PRACTICE GENEROSITY.

GIVE YOURSELF RELATIONALLY TO GOD AND OTHERS
THROUGH CONCRETE ACTS OF GIVING
MORE THAN REQUIRED.

Second, they can begin to follow Jesus as disciples and *practice generosity.*[15] By sharing ourselves with God and others through concrete acts of generosity, we become transformed as people. The antidote to greed isn't to get more; the antidote to greed is to *give more.* True wealth is not about what we have but what we share.

"Where your treasure is, there your heart will be also," said Jesus (Matthew 6:21). How can we know what we treasure? I once heard a man say, "Show me what you do with your money, and I will show you what you love." Jesus gave up the treasure of heaven to make us his treasure. He treasured *us.* Unless we truly believe that we are Jesus' greatest treasure, we will remain addicted to greed and enslaved to fear.

To follow Jesus, we have to fall out of love with our stuff. Money is mentioned more than 2,300 times in the Bible—the majority of which is expressed in language that warns against the devastating effects of greed. Likewise, the Bible mentions caring for the poor nearly as many times. The message is clear: *What we have is to be shared with those in need.* And while money is a helpful thing to share, *what the world really needs us to share is ourselves.* The world needs us to be reliable friends, proactive neighbors, and attentive family members. Ironically, the more we give to others, the more secure we usually end up feeling. Greed breeds scarcity. Generosity breeds abundance. Concrete acts of sharing, giving, and participating is the way forward for the Five.

I know one Five who was struggling with a deeply personal issue related to their sexuality. They told me, "Friends kept asking me how I was doing but I didn't want to answer because I hadn't wrapped my brain around it all yet. I really wanted to keep ruminating on my own. But eventually I realized I needed to let people in. So the next time a friend asked me how I was doing, I gave them an honest answer. It turns out that what I was going through ended up being a mutual hardship. It became a pivotal moment, not just in our relationship, but in both of our lives as a whole. Time is not infinite. We can't ruminate forever. I need to accept the limitations of time and take action—especially in relationships." This is relational generosity in action.

When the Five practices generosity, their life begins to grow a variety of good fruit. *First, practicing generosity allows them to develop community.* While the Five may still need alone time to recharge, they don't do it excessively. Instead, they move toward people and participate in their lives. As Ecclesiastes 4:9–10 says, "Two are better than one, because they have a good return for their labor: If either of them falls down, one can help the other up. But pity anyone who falls and has no one to help them up." Sow a life of isolation, and you end up alone. Nurture a life of relationship, and you end up with community.

Second, they become responsive to the relational needs of others. Instead of acting like it's every man for himself, the Five learns to give a positive and timely response. Over time, they'll become warmer people who consistently offer words of validation and who try to mirror the speaker's emotions when listening. They'll dig into their own time and money to assist people in need. Indifference is replaced with care.

Finally, they develop an abundance mindset. As the Five participates in the life of other people through generosity, they find that their resources aren't nearly as threatened as they had pessimistically imagined. The world is full of sustenance and abundance. They no longer need to obsessively hoard their emotions, space, energy, time, and money. There is more than enough to go around!

Discipleship: Bible Study and Service

To grow in their discipleship and to protect themselves from falling back into their old way of life, the Five will want to practice spiritual disciplines.[16] The first is *inductive Bible study*—an approach to reading the Scriptures that considers elements such as authorship, intent, historical context, cross references, and implications. The Five may even choose to read commentaries or historical works that provide additional insights into the text. In this way, the Five seeks to nurture their mind with the intention of knowing God with more clarity.

Second, the Five will want to practice the spiritual discipline of *regular service projects*. Whether it's signing up to tutor in an afterschool program or swing a hammer with Habitat for Humanity, doing good deeds gets us out of the maze inside our heads. When we help other people by doing child care at church or serving a meal to someone who is finding assistance in a shelter, we realize that we do indeed have the ability to competently help others. We realize that many people don't need our information so much as they need our presence and our simple, ordinary acts of love.

The False Self won't go away easily or quickly. It loves to hide and adapt. But in time, change is truly possible. As the Five walks in the ways of Jesus, they can live a more abundant life full of flourishing relationships.

Each of the types of the Enneagram reflect a different aspect of God's character. *The True Self of the Five reflects God's wisdom and insight.*[17] With God as their source of wisdom, the Five's educational pursuits serve the communities around them. In this

THE FIVE REFLECTS GOD'S WISDOM & INSIGHT.

way, they reflect the eternal wisdom of Jesus himself. The Five invites all of us to sit in awe and wonder as we exclaim, "Oh, the depth of the riches of the wisdom and knowledge of God!" (Romans 11:33).

Practical Tips for the Five

1. Remember that "never enough" breeds "never enough." What you believe is true will shape you. Being generous breeds contentment and gratitude.

2. Catch yourself withdrawing. Notice when you may be pulling back from people when they communicate they want or need you to be present.

3. Create rhythms to share yourself with others. Being vulnerable requires practice. Add time to your calendar to share yourself with others.

4. Practice mirroring others. Research the effects of the "still face experiment" and learn to practice empathetic body language.[18] Facial expressions help bonding.

5. Get in your body. More than any other type, the Five can disconnect from their body. Enjoy life by exercising, feeling sensations, and taking action.

6. Move forward instead of inward. Avoid getting stuck in analysis paralysis by setting deadlines for decisions, talking through the process, and taking action.

CHAPTER 10

TYPE SIX
THE LOYALIST

*Your safety comes from the presence of
God, not the absence of danger.*

My friend Alex used to be a freight train conductor. He handled things like ensuring that the train followed safety rules and practices, kept it on schedule, oversaw all the paperwork, and did some of the grunt work of coupling and uncoupling the cars. He was the details guy who also knew how to get his hands dirty.

One night, as their train was traveling from Louisville to Nashville, a horrible ice storm hit. The crossing gates that warned traffic of approaching trains all froze, leaving drivers in danger of being hit by a train. In the middle of nowhere in the rolling hills of Kentucky, the engineer stopped the train to allow Alex to get out and mark the upcoming intersection with flares.

As they attempted to restart the train, they realized they had a problem. The mile-and-a-half-long train was resting over several hills, making the weight distribution awkward and uneven. As the engineer attempted to restart the train, a coupler connecting two cars suddenly snapped, breaking the train into two parts. As Alex approached the back half of the train to survey the damage, he realized it had come to rest on a bridge one hundred feet above a rushing river. So, here was Alex—at three in the morning in the middle of an ice storm in the middle of nowhere—on top of a bridge attempting to repair a train.

Here's why Alex was the right man for this scenario: Alex had checked the weather forecast ahead of time and brought appropriate work-clothing for a variety of weather—including ice accumulation. He had packed an extra-large tool bag that had the necessary tools for repairing a broken coupler. At one point, he had strapped his belt around the coupler to hold it in place as he repaired it, only to have the belt snap in two. Guess who had also packed a spare belt?

Alex arrived in Nashville with an intact train and warm clothes because of his preparations. If you're like Alex—prepared, reliable, and gifted at anticipating problems—you might be a Six.

True Self

At their best, the Six is faithful, loyal, and committed. Their "yes" is "yes," and their "no" is "no." They are dependable, and they take commitments seriously. Of all the types, the Six is the most organized and prepared. They are naturally systematic and create policies and methods to ensure reliable outcomes. Whether it is paperwork, appointments, schedules, or plans, the Six excels at detailed preparation. When something is entrusted to them, they care for it with responsibility and reliability. While other types are

prone to give rise to conflict and then abandon the other party as punishment, the Six confronts problems but stays committed, thus providing the stability to endure relational hardships.

The Six always seems prepared for any crisis that may arise. They often have emergency supplies nearby—bandages, extra snacks, important paperwork, or even weapons. I once helped a Six move to a new home. In the process of helping them pack, I found a half dozen weapons hidden throughout their house. When I got in their car, I found yet another. Like I said, they're always prepared.

Because of their ability to forecast potential problems and plan for them, I sometimes think of the Six like a security guard. They're on alert for threats against the people and causes they care about, and they show love to the rest of us by creating secure, dependable environments.

The Six brings their deep loyalty to their relationship with God. They dedicate themselves to a lifestyle formed by the rhythms of Jesus and are often deeply involved with their church community. The Six often feels a special resonance with the covenant nature of God. They see in themselves echoes of the God who makes permanent promises and upholds them, even at great personal sacrifice. Because of their loyalty and commitment, the Six does not easily give up on their faith. In their desire to provide secure and dependable environments for people, they give the world a small foretaste of the security of the heaven that is to come.

False Self

When the Six is unhealthy, they overidentify with always being prepared. They're like a security guard who hasn't slept in three days but refuses to go home and get some rest. Their life becomes marked by frantic anxiety and hypervigilance. When they envision the future, it usually ends in an apocalypse. Everyone is sick, everyone is dead, and somehow the planet explodes. This

catastrophic thinking causes the Six to become "stuck" on high alert, forever forecasting danger. They become worried that each person and scenario they encounter is a trojan horse that contains unforeseen threats. They become reluctant, wary, and suspicious of others. To protect themselves and the people they love in case danger were to arise, they just make a few contingency plans. And backup plans for those plans. And backup plans for those plans. Some people use the word *paranoid* to describe this type of behavior.

Constantly "bracing themselves for impact" causes the Six to become uptight and rigid. They become hypervigilant about danger, details, and follow-through and are unable to relax or to allow others to relax. They feel there is always more to be done, more unforeseen threats to guard against, and more items on their mental checklist to fulfill. This heightened anxiousness and pushy vigilance become a challenging dynamic in their relationships. When other people just want to kick up their feet for a moment, the Six is certain that to do so will somehow result in cancer.

They give trust to others and to authorities, but their hypersensitivity to danger causes them to take back all their trust if their ideals are not met. They can have a push-pull dynamic in relationships—full of certainty one moment and unflinching suspicion and mistrust the next. They doubt others, but they doubt themselves most of all. They are uncertain about their own motives, whether they can trust their own convictions or are capable of taking the correct action. They're hard on themselves, often trying to decide whether their own perspective is trustworthy. Unsure of how to find a safe way forward, many Sixes have a history of starting and stopping—often with a good excuse for why their previously chosen path wasn't trustworthy. AJ Sherrill says that Sixes "find it easier to question than to act."[1]

They bring this push-pull dynamic to their relationship with God. The Six can be filled with a serene trusting faith one day and gripped with crippling doubt the next. They doubt their own ability to hear the voice of God, to understand the Scriptures, or to consistently believe the Christian faith. They doubt the presence of God inside them that speaks to them moment by moment. They bring their pushy vigilance to God, where they demand that he fulfill their ideals or else they'll suspect the whole Christian faith is a scam. Fear tosses their faith around like the waves of the sea as they desperately try to locate the nearest life raft.

Childhood and Adolescence: Danger and Unpredictability

The childhood theme of the Six is *danger and unpredictability*. Many Sixes describe their childhood as one where the possibility of harm was realistic and ongoing. These threats could have come from fam-ily, friends, or circumstances. We may sometimes want to poke fun at their worry or paranoia, but the truth is that many Sixes experienced deeply distressing or disturbing experiences of some kind in their early years of life. Some Sixes may have grown up in war-torn countries, in neighborhoods with drive-by shootings, or in homes

THE CHILDHOOD THEME OF THE SIX IS
DANGER & UNPREDICTABILITY.

with alcoholic parents. Maybe Mom had a mental illness or their brother died in a car accident. Maybe Dad did something unmen-tionably horrific to them, or they ended up dating a guy in high school who psychologically terrorized them.

Other Sixes don't report trauma of this magnitude but instead point to the unpredictable expectations of their community. One Six shared a story about her life in middle school, where friends abandoned her without warning—accepting her one day and bullying her the next. It's hard to feel relationally secure when you realize that people are unpredictable and friends may abandon you. The Six felt surrounded by threats and feared that no one in their life could truly protect them. Naturally, this created an anxious atmosphere where the "code red" alarm was normal.

All of this shaped the Six's view of the world as being a fundamentally dangerous and unpredictable place and impacted their ability to trust their own instincts. Being unable to adequately forecast and protect themselves from danger and unpredictability, the Six came to believe that *it's not okay to trust or depend on yourself.*[2] It's an unfair burden. How can a kid predict when Dad is going to lose his job, Mom is going to have a stroke, or their shoelace will come untied just as they walk onstage causing them to fall and split open their forehead?

The Six searches for their security in established authorities and predictable guidelines. Clear leadership, regulated protocols, and proven pathways ease their uncertain mind. Many Sixes come from families of Sixes. As their own authority figures said things like, "Look out"; "Don't run"; "That doesn't sound like a good idea"; and "I think you better let me handle that for you," the young Six learned to doubt their own competency while becoming overly reliant on the judgments of the adults in the room. The worries of their caregivers were thrown onto the child, who then learns to worry as well. For a lot of Sixes, the apple doesn't fall far from the tree.

Because they can't depend on their own skills and judgments to survive a dangerous world, the Six searches for outside assistance. The thing they search for is also what they fear they won't find—creating a basic fear of being *without support and guidance.*[3] They're scared that they will be left to navigate this dangerous world all alone. They're scared to trust their own internal guidance system, which is one of the main reasons the Six is so loyal and often willing to go down with the ship. It's better to die among friends than it is to die alone.

This fear fosters self-doubt, which makes authority figures, structures, allies, and guiding beliefs extremely attractive for the Six. However, the Six often tests those closest to them by questioning their motives, reliability, and faithfulness. A Six who doesn't know who to trust ends up ping-ponging back and forth between whatever influence is momentarily pressing upon them. This is why the Six is often called a "bundle of opposites." They can rapidly oscillate between cowardice and courage, faith and doubt, compliance and rebellion, ease and vigilance, running from fear and attacking fear.

If you take a kid and raise them in a dangerous and unpredictable environment, then nurture the idea that they can't trust their own instincts, you end up with someone who experiences a lot of *fear and anxiety*.[4] While these worries can attach to specific scenarios, the experience is often generalized. Many Sixes can be wary of engaging with people or situations that are unfamiliar to them. They may be easily spooked or fidgety or struggle with racing thoughts. While fatigued from their hypervigilance, they can often struggle to relax. Their anxiety manifests as authoritatively alternating among compliance, control, and community, or, as Beatrice Chestnut says, the Six deals with anxiety through "fight, flight, or friends."[5]

Inside their loyal, dedicated heart is a kid who wants a loving authority figure to tell them, *"You are safe and secure in my care."*[6] They want someone to stand between them and danger. They just want to know that when the chaos hits the fan, someone will be there to shield them from the shrapnel. They want to be swept up into the bosom of someone who is one part bulletproof and one part

THE SIX WANTS TO BE SECURE.

sage. Then they can finally rest, safe in the presence of a loving guardian.

Considering the story they've lived, it's easy to see their core desire: *the Six wants to be secure.*[7] They want their anxiety replaced with calm, their insecurity replaced with confidence, and their uncertainty replaced with trust. They want to be held firmly where they won't be lost, abandoned, or alone. They want a place and a people where they belong and feel secure.

However, when this good desire to be secure is unsatisfied, it eventually morphs into something harmful.

Nurturing Your False Self: Mistaking Safety for Security

Sometimes the difference between where we aim and where we end up is only a few degrees. If you're going to the grocery store, a few degrees don't matter too much. If you're going to the moon, you

WHAT IS THE SIX WILLING TO SACRIFICE?

FEELING CAREFREE & RELAXED

TRUSTING GOD & OTHER PEOPLE

TRUSTING THEIR OWN IDEAS

THE IDOL OF THE LOYALIST: SAFETY

had better double-check those calculations. Just a few degrees in the wrong direction, and you're on a one-way trip to another solar system.

The difference between what the Six wants and what they settle for can seem so small and so insignificant that at first it seems nearly identical. The Six wants to be secure, but *they settle for the false idol of safety.* Being the bundle of opposites they are, the Six can worship at the idol of safety in two different ways. The first way they can feel safe from threats is by retreating and shielding themselves. The second way they can feel safe is by hunting for threats and attacking first. Whether retreating or charging, the goal is the same—to get more safety.

The problem with this approach becomes clearer when we ask ourselves, *How much safety is enough safety?* Is it enough that we're generally happy and healthy and have each other? Is it enough to live in a neighborhood with a low-crime rate? Do we also need an alarm system? Do we also need a dog? Do we also need to close all the shades? Do we also need to hire a security guard? Do we also need to avoid the neighbors because they seem a little odd? Do we need to avoid *everyone?*

Or the opposite: Is it enough that there is relative peace right now with no evidence that anything is wrong? Do we also need to provoke people to see if they're hiding anything? Do we also need to assume that everyone is against us until they prove otherwise? Do we also need to attack before they get a chance to? Do we need to fight everyone? Whether the Six is saying, *Don't run! You'll fall down!* or *Next time, you'd better punch them back!* both paths idolize safety.

As all idols do, the idol of safety demands sacrifices. The idol of safety requires the Six to sacrifice feeling carefree and relaxed, trusting God and other people, and their own ideas and beliefs. The Six becomes plagued by doubts and learns not to trust anyone—including themselves.

What happens when the Six puts their hope in the idol of safety? They grow the deadly sin of *fear.*[8] When we are tortured by fear, we're scared of everything.

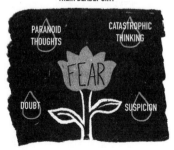

HOW DOES THE SIX NURTURE THEIR DEADLY SIN?

PARANOID THOUGHTS

CATASTROPHIC THINKING

FEAR

DOUBT

SUSPICION

We're scared of being betrayed and of betraying others. We're scared of being deceived, of being thrown out of the group, of being caught off guard. We're scared of being trapped, of being attacked, of being manipulated. We end up oscillating between cowardice and premature attacks, between running from fear and recklessly attacking it.

The world *is* a dangerous place. There is plenty of evidence to support why the Six is often afraid. However, the Six makes the mistake of believing their catastrophic thinking is realistic. Real threats and imagined threats begin to have the same plausibility. The Six becomes locked into anxiety about *possible* threats and danger as opposed to responding only to *actual* threats and danger. Fear becomes a motivator as well as an excuse for bad behavior.

To cope with danger and unpredictability and to maintain their self-image of being loyal and prepared, the Six defends themselves through *projection*[9]—a defense mechanism in which a person brings their own fearful biases into a relationship and treats the other person as if those biases are true. The Six is particularly compelled to project their own thoughts, emotions, motivations, or behaviors onto others that are unacceptable, unwanted, or disowned. For example, a Six may accuse someone of being unreliable when the Six themselves has been unreliable. They may refuse to go to any social gatherings they're invited to by coworkers but then accuse those coworkers of being cliquish. They perceive others as threats and then respond to those people as threats—even when the evidence does not support their interpretation. Perception is treated as reality. They can sabotage relationships by thrusting their anxiety, doubts, and suspicions on others, which can drive people away and ultimately create a self-fulfilling prophecy.

It's important to remember how scary life was for a Six when they were a kid. The world felt dangerous and unpredictable. True threats seemed to show up unexpectedly, and the adults in their life either struggled to shield them from danger or were even the sources of that danger. One Six told me he saw over a dozen friends killed before he graduated from high school. Another said that Dad would come home drunk and sit next to their bed crying. We may roll our eyes at their anxiety or hesitation, but the reality is that a lot of Sixes have been through some serious stuff. The truth is that we all have things we're scared of. Things from our past haunt us. Fear is either a shield or a sword in our relationships. We either hide behind it or use it against people. Fear stifles our ability to trust. Without trust, we're on our own.

What makes fear so deadly is that it feels familiar and natural. The Six comes to believe that *the dangers of the world justify my fear*. Their anxiety, worry, and doubt are justified because of the threats that surround them. They believe that both real and projected threats deserve equal amounts of fear. This allows the Six to confuse acting cowardly or recklessly with acting responsibly. Sometimes even sin is reframed as a necessary evil in the pursuit of safety.

Your Encounter with Jesus, the True Loyalist

As the Six encounters Jesus, they discover that he empathizes with their pain. *Like the Six, Jesus' life from birth to death was marked by danger, threats, and unpredictability.* He understands what it means to live in a threatening and dangerous world that wants to harm

him. Threats were lurking around every corner in Jesus' life. In response to Jesus' birth, King Herod ordered that every infant male under the age of two be killed. His parents fled their own country to escape. As an adult, religious leaders regularly threatened him or attempted to stone him. His friends bailed on him. Eventually, politicians, religious leaders, and crowds of strangers

LIKE THE SIX, JESUS' LIFE FROM BIRTH TO DEATH WAS MARKED BY DANGER, THREATS, AND UNPREDICTABILITY.

worked together to successfully crucify him. We could never again say that God doesn't understand what it's like to feel small and fragile. When Jesus talked about anxiety, it wasn't from a far-off isolation chamber. Jesus lived in the center of the storm, and he knows the danger that this world brings with it.

Jesus also shows his authority over life and his mastery of relationships. *Jesus affirms the True Self of the Six by being faithful.* He

LIKE THE SIX, JESUS WAS FAITHFUL.

demonstrated unrelenting fidelity to both God and people. Unlike us, who are so often a bag of mixed motives and hidden agendas, Jesus was pure goodness. His loyalty to God and to the truth are unparalleled. He did not destroy God's law but came to fulfill it (Matthew 5:17). Like the Six, Jesus valued the covenant he made.

Like a Six, Jesus was obedient. When we hear the word *obedience*, it can conjure up images of robots or dogs, but it may be better to think of it in terms of the enactment of a plan. The Trinity put together a plan for the rescue and redemption of humanity, and Jesus came to this earth to carry out his part in that plan. Jesus tells us, "I have come down from heaven not to do my will but to do the will of him who sent me" (John 6:38). The goal of his obedience was to deliver us from bondage, protect us from the power of death, and give us eternal security with God (Romans 5:19). The Son submitted to the Father because he trusted his plan.

However, Jesus also confronts the False Self of the Six by telling people not to fear but to trust. Having just received the news that his daughter had died, a synagogue leader named Jairus was in shock and grieving. And then we read this: "Overhearing what they said, Jesus told him, 'Don't be afraid; just believe'" (Mark 5:36). I don't know about you, but if anyone were to say that to me after my kid died, I'd probably throw a punch or two. But Jesus does the unthinkable.

He miraculously raises her to life.[10] In the famous Sermon on the Mount, Jesus tells his listeners to seek God's kingdom above everything else and then concludes by imploring them, "Therefore do not worry about tomorrow, for tomorrow will worry about itself" (Matthew 6:34). Our capacity to trust decides our capacity for intimacy. If we want to be close to God and others, we have to learn to trust them.

Jesus didn't wait for things to be safe before he took action. In fact, Jesus reminds his followers to anticipate danger and threats. He tells them, "If the world hates you, keep in mind that it hated me first" (John 15:18). He doesn't sugarcoat reality. We're told that even when the crowds celebrated him, he "would not entrust himself to them, for he knew all people" (John 2:24). Jesus was street-smart. Yet even though he knew their impure motives and their forthcoming betrayal, he continued to do miracles and heal their sick. "In this world you will

JESUS CONFRONTS THE SIX BY NOT WAITING FOR THINGS TO BE SAFE BEFORE TAKING ACTION.

have trouble," he said, "But take heart! I have overcome the world" (John 16:33). Danger was never a valid reason for sinful action or cowardice.

How did Jesus display faithfulness and obedience and yet never succumb to the deadly sin of fear? Why didn't Jesus *need* to be safe? *Jesus believed he was safe in his Father's care.* He believed the safest place he could be was within the will of God. In Gethsemane, Jesus knew what awaited him—horrible relational and physical anguish. He was going to be separated from his Father for the first time, abandoned by his friends, and tortured by people he loved. We're told he was so distraught that "his sweat was like drops of blood falling to the ground" (Luke 22:44). And yet he relinquished his control to the Father: "Father, if you are willing, take this cup from me; yet not my will, but yours be done" (Luke 22:42). When the world had gone dark and all hope seemed lost, Jesus had to decide whether or not his Father deserved his trust.

Redeeming Your True Self: From Safety to Courage

As the Six revisits the story of their life, they're met with troubling memories of feeling alone and scared. They've lived as wary participants in an ever-changing world. For their entire life they've lived with the belief that they must be hypervigilant in order to survive the threats that surround them.

THE SIX IS GIVEN THE GOOD NEWS,
"YOU ARE SAFE AND SECURE IN MY CARE."

What they really wanted was just to be secure. They needed someone to find them in their greatest moment of fear and take care of them. To the Six, God bends low and scoops up the child inside. He meets them in their terror, their anxiety, and their insecurities. To the Six, God says, *"You are safe in my care."* The Six finds in the gospel the very thing they are looking for—to be relationally safe and secure.

Paul's letter to the Romans meditates on God's love for us. "If God is for us, who can be against us?" (Romans 8:31). Our God is *with us* and *for us*. We can declare, along with Paul, that we are convinced that nothing can ever separate us from God's love. Neither death nor life, neither angels nor demons, neither our fears for today nor our worries about tomorrow—not even the powers of hell—can separate us from God's love (Romans 8:38–39). Nothing in all of creation—including our own doubts, anxieties, or brokenness—can separate us from the loving presence of God.

The Six frequently believes that people cannot be trusted because of their sin, mixed motives, and limited capabilities. God is not like humanity. As James reminds us, God "does not change like shifting shadows" (1:17). Throughout the Scriptures, we are told that "God is faithful" (1 Corinthians 10:13), that "in him there is no darkness at all" (1 John 1:5), and that he "is not slow in keeping his promise" (2 Peter 3:9). He tells his people, "I have loved you with an everlasting love" (Jeremiah 31:3). In Christ, the Six is safe in the care of God.

Jesus doesn't tell the Six, "Calm down already!" He tells them to bring their burdens to him, to cast their cares on his shoulders. Jesus will tend to their needs and their worries. He does not promise to fulfill their idealistic standards of safety. He promises to be present. He promises that there will be troubles, but that there is also a plan. He promises that he will give them everything they need for today. In the end, no threats can win. No power can swallow them. No one can snatch them from the hands of God.

What might happen if the Six believes this is true? What will happen if the Holy Spirit saturates their mind with the truth that they are secure in God's care? They can follow Jesus as a disciple by abandoning their old way of seeing and by taking on his vision for life.

First, it would benefit the Six to recognize the damage done by their fixation on fear. What relationships were kept at bay? What dreams were never attempted? What goals were abandoned? Which people bore the brunt of the blame? Unless we grieve the damage caused by our participation in our deadly sin, it will continue to hold power over us.

Second, to counteract their fear, the Six will want to practice the virtue of *courage*. Believing they are safe in God's loving care, the Six can stop using their hypervigilance and safety protocols to feel secure. Jesus tells us, "Your Father knows what you need before you ask him" (Matthew 6:8). The Six no longer needs to obsess about things they may have overlooked; they can be secure in the knowledge that nothing slips past the ever-attentive presence of God. As the Six becomes aware of God's presence and activity, they can stop living in fear.

Courage is not the alleviation of fear. Courage is the ability to be scared of something and to confront it anyway. American poet Karle Wilson Baker wrote, "Courage is fear that has said its prayers."[11] For this reason, the Six is the most courageous of all the types. The Six is more aware of the threats, dangers, and unpredictability in the world and yet they choose to step forward. To walk into danger with a firm trust in God is to break the chains of fear. As my friend Lindsey Lewis says, "The Six is invited to move from the fear of 'what if?' to the courage of 'even if.'"

Like all of the virtues within the Enneagram, courage is a habit. It is developed only by *doing* courageous acts. We cannot choose cowardice and courage simultaneously. We stand at the fork in the road and must choose one. As theologian Mary Daly said, "You learn to swim by swimming. You learn courage by couraging."[12] One way to become more courageous is to be fully present in the current moment. Becoming aware of their bodily sensations, their emotions, the people around them, and the Holy Spirit

TO COUNTERACT FEAR,
PRACTICE COURAGE.

AVOID COWARDICE AND ATTACK, CHOOSING INSTEAD TO
TRUST GOD'S PRESENCE IN AND AROUND YOU.

inside them will help give the Six an accurate perception of their life. By engaging their discomfort zone and exposing themselves to things that intimidate them, the Six will begin to see they are more capable than they thought and their apocalyptic concerns less warranted than they imagined.

I know one Six who was engaged to a man. As someone who was wary of trusting herself, she was initially attracted to his confidence and self-assurance. However, as the relationship progressed, he became verbally abusive and manipulative, eventually falsely accusing her of betrayal and telling her, "If you ever left me, no one would ever love you like I do. You would end up alone." In the end, she overcame her fear through the courageous act of leaving him. She did not end up alone. She went on to build a happy, healthy life without him.

When the Six practices courage, their life begins to grow a variety of good fruit. *First, practicing courage allows the Six to experience peace.* The courage to avoid both rigid compliance and domineering control will allow the Six to rest, not in protocol, but in the presence of God. By cultivating an awareness of God's presence, their anxiety can be replaced with peace. The exhausted security guard can finally take a nap.

Second, they learn to trust. The Six can move past skepticism and mistrust into healthy trust. Trust—even imperfect, uncertain trust—can reap a harvest if we are willing to ask ourselves, *What would I do if I truly trusted right now?* The action of trust is courage in the flesh. Proverbs tells us, "Trust in the LORD with all your heart and lean not on your own understanding; in all your ways submit to him, and he will make your paths straight" (3:5–6).

Finally, they develop self-confidence. The Six learns that they are actually far more skilled, competent, and capable than they realized. They learn to trust their own judgment and their own ability to discern the Holy Spirit speaking to them. Maybe their internal guidance system isn't as broken as they feared.

Discipleship: Singing, Journaling, and Memorizing

To protect themselves from falling back into their old way of relating, the Six will want to practice three primary spiritual disciplines. *First, they will want to sing with other believers.* AJ Sherrill says, "Singing with others solidifies that they are not alone in their convictions."[13] My wife, a Six, tells me every Sunday morning, "I want to get to church early. I don't want to miss any of the singing. It's my favorite part."

Second, the Six will want to journal. Journaling provides a safe space for the Six to release their unfiltered worries and anxieties. By writing down their fears, the Six is able to sort out their thoughts and discern which ones need further care through prayer, conversation, or action.

The third discipline the Six will benefit from is Scripture memorization. By memorizing Scripture, the Six acquires tools to combat worry, lies, and fear. They will feel more equipped to face life's challenges, no matter the context or circumstances. As they recall Scripture throughout the day, they become more aware of God's constant presence with them.[14]

Change doesn't come easily. We often have a million excuses waiting in the wings for why changing can even be dangerous. However, as the Six receives more deeply the good news that they are secure in God's care and as they practice the virtue of courage, their life will transform.

THE SIX REFLECTS GOD'S
LOYALTY & COVENANT.

Each of the traits of the Enneagram—when healthy—reflect a different aspect of God's character. *The True Self of the Six reflects God's faithfulness and covenant.*[15] Second Timothy 2:13 tells us, "If we are faithless, he remains faithful, for he cannot disown himself." When the Six is faithful, courageous, steadfast, and sacrificial, they show the world that God is too. While the rest of the world is often abandoning their post to chase the newest, shiniest things, the Six stays true to their commitments. The Six helps us see that God makes promises and always fulfills them—because he loves us and wants good for us.

Practical Tips for the Six

1. **Remember God's faithfulness.** Note specific ways God has been faithful to you in the past and specific times you have survived previous crises.
2. **Acknowledge the positive aspects of ideas and plans rather than just the flaws.** Don't just poke holes. Be vocal with your praise and optimism.
3. **Be willing to take appropriate risks.** Courage is a muscle that can only grow when it's used. If you don't take risks, courage will atrophy and you'll be back where you started.
4. **Be careful about overidentifying with any one group.** Recognize that every group has pros and cons, virtues and flaws.
5. **Practice independence.** You are not an incompetent idiot. You don't need everyone else's opinions before you act. Do something solo.
6. **Recognize your bias.** If you look long enough for evidence to confirm your fears, you'll eventually find it. Don't create self-fulfilling prophecies.

CHAPTER 11

TYPE SEVEN
THE ENTHUSIAST

———————————

Your satisfaction comes from God's
abundance, not from indulgence.

I was having lunch with my friend Kyle. I mentioned that some friends of ours from Africa would be in England soon for a vacation and I was thinking about trying to go visit them. Before I'd had a chance to fully consider the weight of my proposition, Kyle responded, "Yes! Let's do it. My family and I will meet you there!"

This is how, four months later, I found myself driving a sports car through the countryside of Oxfordshire. Every day held a different adventure. One day, we visited a village where we passed a tobacco shop. Kyle convinced us to buy handcrafted pipes from a local artisan. Upon discovering that another friend of ours would be in the same village in just a few weeks, Kyle bought an extra pipe. We then went to Winston Churchill's childhood home nearby, where Kyle hid the pipe on the three-hundred-year-old palace grounds. We then sent our friend obscure clues to find it. (Three weeks later when he visited, he did find it.)

Another day, Kyle encouraged the nine children from our families to write a play for all of us to perform at the five-hundred-year-old farmhouse where we were staying. To perform his role as the king, Kyle wrapped himself in a red blanket as his mantle, used a ladle as his scepter, and strapped an upside-down napkin holder to his head for his crown. He transformed from being an adult to a kid pretending to be an adult. The children ate it up.

Every day, Kyle would drive us to a nearby village to go grocery shopping. More specifically, he'd take us to go buy one of every type of candy we couldn't find here in the United States, and then we'd spend the evening eating it all until only a pile of wrappers remained.

How did I end up in England trying one of every type of exotic candy we could find, performing a children's play in a five-hundred-year-old farmhouse, and creating a scavenger hunt on the grounds of a palace? Because Kyle is a Seven. If you enjoy having fun, celebrating life, and living with a sense of wonder, you might be a Seven too.

True Self

At their best, the Seven is enthusiastic, lively, and engaging. If you've ever been around a kid on Christmas morning, you've experienced a bit of the contagious wonder and enthusiasm that a Seven radiates. (Good news for the rest of us: joy is contagious.) They love to encour-

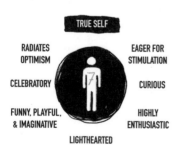

age others, celebrate milestones, and share experiences. They're excited to be alive and eager to explore the wonders of the world. They're forward-thinking, optimistic people who enjoy new and spontaneous experiences. They're almost always up for a good adventure.

In many ways, the Seven embodies the inner child hidden in all of us. While many of us lost our inner child somewhere along the perilous mountain pass of our teen years, the Seven brought theirs into adulthood as a friend. Every day is a "Take Your Inner Child to Work" day with a Seven. Playful and fun-loving, the Seven brings delight and enthusiasm into their relationships. They love to be lighthearted, to laugh, and to tell funny stories. They remind us that despite the pain and evil around us, the world is still deserving of our childlike wonder. Of all the types, they often have the strongest imaginations.

As a member of the Head Triad, the Seven has a fast and busy mind that is often seeking stimulation. They're naturally curious people and can surprise the people around them by joking around one moment and then asking deep, profound, emotionally weighty questions the next. A mature Seven can quiet their joking in order to discuss serious matters and hard topics with other people. Additionally, the healthy Seven sticks to their commitments and can endure through difficult and painful situations. Their optimism befriends realism, their joy befriends their sorrow.

The Seven brings these characteristics to their relationship with God. They feel a natural connection to God amid sensual experiences such as climbing a mountain, experiencing an expressive worship service, or eating a delicious meal. Their prayer life often reflects hope and wonder at the movement of God. They often participate in missions or ministry with genuine excitement that they can be part of God's ever-expanding kingdom and can hold to the belief that God is always doing new things.

False Self

When unhealthy, the inner child of the Seven takes over. They overidentify with their need to avoid pain. They avoid pain at all costs and use their fantasies, hobbies, or joke telling as a means of

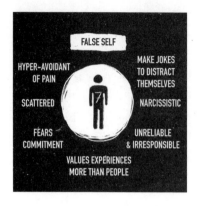

escaping discomfort. Of all the types, the unhealthy Seven is the most sensitive to pain and has the lowest tolerance for emotional discomfort. Because commitments carry the risk of being stuck in a painful situation, the Seven will often resist a sense of obligation about small things such as attending a social event or big things such as getting married. They prefer to stay uncommitted and free to explore their whimsical impulses. As a result, others sometimes experience them as unreliable and irresponsible. When fun is king, commitment feels like an enemy.

They can be easily distracted and sometimes suffer from monkey mind—swinging from topic to topic due to an incessant mental chattering and internal busyness. One Seven says they suffer from ADOSD: "Attention-deficit . . . ooh, shiny! disorder." In social situations, they can hardly stand when a conversation has become too serious or too tense and will often make jokes to lighten the mood or change the topic to something more desirable. If that doesn't work, they'll simply abandon ship in search of people or activities that are more entertaining.

Of all the types, the unhealthy Seven is the most prone to addiction—a means to numb their anxiety and fear of being in pain. In these cases, the primary trusting relationship in their life becomes their object of addiction instead of people. This addiction can come in many forms—food, sex, drugs, traveling, social media. People can sometimes be used as pathways to experiences, leaving others feeling devalued and pressured to entertain the Seven.

This self-referential way of thinking can become narcissistic, where the Seven sees every opportunity, experience, and relationship only as it relates to them. Our solar system orbits the sun, but the unhealthy Seven thinks everything orbits around them. This selfishness carries with it a demanding pushiness and sense of entitlement. In this way, they can be juvenile and act younger than their chronological age, leaving them naive to the real world.

The unhealthy Seven carries this disposition into their relationship with God and others. The Seven may enjoy a rambunctious worship service but avoid committing to serve at their church each week. They may enjoy a great road trip with their spouse but become irritated when difficult topics come up in conversation in the car. God and others are only useful when they're exciting. When the fun ceases, the unhealthy Seven begins to look for an escape hatch to find the next shiny adventure.

Childhood and Adolescence: Prolonged Childhood and Loss of Paradise

The childhood theme of the Seven is *prolonged childhood and loss of paradise*. A lot of Sevens look back on their childhood with fondness. However, because of their tendency to put a positive spin on things, it can be difficult to discern how happy the experience really was. The line between memory and fantasy can get blurry.

Some Sevens enjoyed their childhood until some type of deeply painful event occurred. Maybe their parents divorced or got seriously ill. Other Sevens

THE CHILDHOOD THEME OF THE SEVEN IS PROLONGED CHILDHOOD & LOSS OF PARADISE.

can't recall a specific incident so much as a general sense that their childhood was slipping away. In the same way that middle-aged people are often sad to leave behind the first half of their life as they enter the second half, some Sevens are sad to leave their childhood behind and become young adults. Growing up involves a loss of innocence, more responsibilities, and puberty. It's not exactly heaven. One Seven told me his birthdays made him sad because he just wanted to stay a kid. If we had to choose, Peter Pan would clearly be the patron saint of the Seven. In an attempt to reclaim their innocence, many Sevens coped with this newfound threat by attempting to go back in time to an earlier stage of development where they were happy, safe, and content. It's like a midlife crisis for tweens. Instead of buying a sports car to feel younger, they talk like a five-year-old and act blissfully aloof.

Some Sevens felt caught between a pushy, domineering parent and a soft, permissive parent. The Seven usually avoided their domineering parent and bonded with their permissive one—often through indulgence and escapism. Ice cream and television are going to beat out chores every time. Many Sevens felt frustrated because they weren't nurtured enough, always needing more. The Seven learned that being direct about their needs could sometimes create conflict with their parents, so they developed more strategic, indirect ways to get their needs met—by being funny, charming, enthusiastic, and persistent. If you've ever been around a Seven who has their mind set on something, they're similar to an adorable puppy who won't let go of your sock. It's hard to be mad at them (and they know it).

In their youth, these experiences of prolonged childhood and a loss of paradise led the Seven to subconsciously conclude *it's not okay to depend on others for anything.*[1] The loss of their idyllic childhood and sense of paradise proved to the Seven that no one else was going to take care of them, so they were going to have to take matters into their own hands. The Seven learned that by using the power of their imagination and their upbeat energy, they could transform bad outcomes into more pleasant ones. They become independent people who push for their imaginative ideas to become reality. If they want something, they're just going to go get it.

Between feeling kidnapped from their childhood and their

dislike of depending on other people, the Seven became *afraid of being deprived or trapped in pain.*[2] Of course, pain is a spectrum. On the one end are childbirth, abuse, and broken legs. On the other end are missing out on things and working in a cubicle. The Seven is scared of the entire spectrum. While they're afraid of momentary pain, they can become downright petrified of long-term pain. Living in a state of agony from which they can't escape is a fate worse than death. I knew one Seven who had a recurring nightmare that he was walking down the street when a wood chipper would suddenly suck him in feetfirst before breaking down halfway. He would spend the rest of his dream trapped and unable to escape. Either through deprivation or entrapment, the Seven fears they will be left suffering and wanting.

If you take a kid and force them to grow up before they're ready, make them afraid to depend on other people, and make them feel they might be trapped in pain they can't escape from, you end up with someone who is experiencing a lot of *fear and anxiety.*[3] Their minds race as they try to find something pleasant to soothe their anxiety. Their bodies fidget to warn them that they're near their threshold for pain. When the Seven can't see a clear path forward to a happier place, they go into a state of distress. Though they come across as lighthearted, under the surface many Sevens are running for their lives, trying to escape the unpleasant feelings that nip at their heels.

Inside their vivacious, enthusiastic heart is just a kid who wants someone to understand their dreams and their fears and tell them, *"You will be taken care of."*[4] They want someone to scoop them up, carry them out of the maze they're lost in, and take them out for ice cream. If someone could meet their needs, they wouldn't have to feel the ache of longing anymore. If someone could heal their wounds, they wouldn't be in pain. Their anxiety could be replaced with tranquility and contentment.

The Seven *wants to be happy.*[5] When we're happy, we're content.

THE SEVEN WANTS TO BE HAPPY.

We have no wants or needs. Our hunger is satisfied. When we share our happiness with others, we feel more connected to one another. Happiness motivates us, energizes us, and makes us more productive. When we're happy, time freezes. We suddenly take notice of the beauty of life—grandparents, frozen ponds, fresh strawberries, warm chai. When we're happy, we expect little and are surprised by much. Happiness undoes the power of pain. If something makes us happy, we'll return to it a thousand times over just to get a small taste of joy.

However, somewhere along the way, the Seven's desire for happiness gets amplified and warped into something that ends up bringing more pain into their life.

Nurturing Your False Self: Mistaking Indulgence for Happiness

In their quest to find a path to happiness, they don't turn to God, but rather *they settle for the false idol of pleasure.* Why? Because they can't tell the difference between happiness and pleasure. The Seven asks themselves, *Where am I?* and now they have an answer: *I'm not*

WHAT IS THE SEVEN WILLING TO SACRIFICE?

FEELING SATISFIED · DEPTH IN RELATIONSHIPS · DISCIPLINE & FOCUS

THE IDOL OF THE ENTHUSIAST
PLEASURE

sure, but at least I feel good. Historically, this outlook would be referred to as hedonism—the belief that the highest aim of life is the satisfaction of desires. Decisions become based on the goal of decreasing pain and increasing pleasure. When we elevate pleasure as the highest good, pain ends up having no redeeming value.

However, the idol of pleasure comes at a cost and requires sacrifices. The Seven must sacrifice feeling satisfied and fulfilled, developing discipline and focus, and depth in relationships. Sadly, shallow relationships ultimately make for a shallow life.

What happens when the Seven puts their hope in the idol of pleasure? They grow the deadly sin of *gluttony*.[6] While gluttony is often associated with food, it is more helpful to think of this deadly sin as a lifestyle of habitual excess. To be gluttonous is to love physical pleasure so much that we refuse to sacrifice our own gratification. Gluttony whispers to us, *Why delay your desires? Do it now!* Gluttony disguises itself as a solution to stress and anxiety while actually compounding our pain.

HOW DOES THE SEVEN NURTURE THEIR DEADLY SIN?

HABITUALLY EXCESSIVE

ALWAYS SEEKING NEW EXPERIENCES

GLUTTONY

AVOIDS PAIN

VALUES PLEASURE OVER PEOPLE

We spend too much and go into debt. We drink too much and make decisions we regret. We sleep around and wake up feeling hollow. We eat until we don't recognize the person in the mirror. We devour more and leave others with less. We plan for the future and ignore the present. Gluttony infects us with insatiable desire. A little more is almost enough. Excess doesn't fill us with happiness; it empties us of joy.

In many ways, an unhealthy Seven can operate like an addict. For addicts, their substance abuse initially gets them high. Eventually though, they need to take a higher dose to experience the same degree of pleasure they first experienced. In the end, however, the person no longer takes the substance to get high but instead to avoid feeling low. They become dependent. What looked like a door to freedom has turned into a prison cell.

I worked for a homeless shelter and addiction recovery program for nine years. By far, the most common type among the recovering addicts in our community was the Seven. Many of them were some of the funniest and most charismatic people I've ever met. I deeply loved their company and presence. A lot of the guys in our program came from painful childhoods. The truth is that the drugs and the booze and the gambling were actually about fear and anxiety. They initially started drinking or shooting up to escape their pain. Sadly, in doing so, they actually compounded it. The very thing they were afraid of—being trapped in pain—was the very thing they caused.

To cope with their fears of being deprived or trapped in pain, and to protect their idol of pleasure, the Seven defends themselves through *sublimation*[7]—a psychological defense mechanism in which a person puts anything or anyone unpleasant out of awareness. One way the Seven accomplishes this is by attempting to reframe negative situations into something positive, even when it requires downplaying the severity of the circumstance.

I know one Seven whose father died. He was an only child who was especially close to his dad, and I knew he had experienced a devastating loss. However, when I visited him two days later, he made light of it all. He just smiled and said, "I'm actually really happy. I'm just glad he's with Jesus!" As my friend Sam says, "The Seven tends to want to skip from Good Friday to Easter Sunday. They have to learn to sit in the darkness of Holy Saturday."

Don't let the joking and silliness fool you. Many Sevens have a lot of buried pain in their lives. While all of us have a hard time talking about hurtful things we've experienced, it can be especially hard for the Seven. When we probe into their painful memories, some Sevens can find themselves at a total loss for words, flooded with emotion, and unsure of what they're even looking for. Whatever they did experience, it was hurtful enough that they often don't want to revisit it. No matter how it made it into their heart, the message was clear: *Run from pain. You have to take care of yourself. Try to find scraps of happiness where you can.* The problem is that now the Seven can't stop running and can't stop indulging.

What makes gluttony so deadly for the Seven is that it feels familiar and justifiable. Their sin is reframed into something they see as reasonable: *The pain of the world justifies my gluttony.* They believe pleasure exists to offset the weight of pain. Why settle for a life of suffering or boredom when the world has offered so much pleasure to us? Why settle for moderation when we can indulge our desires? Why settle for misery when joy is possible? The Seven confuses their gluttony with joyful celebration.

Your Encounter with Jesus, the True Enthusiast

Jesus empathizes with the pain of the Seven. *Like the Seven, Jesus lost true paradise and experienced a painful world.* Jesus knew the bliss of heaven. Before time existed, he experienced satisfaction, contentment, and joy. When creation became marred by sin, he left behind the comfort of heaven

for our sake. On earth, Jesus cried, grieved, was threatened, and felt excruciating physical pain. Jesus knows what it's like to be disappointed and not receive the things he wanted. More than anyone in all of creation, Jesus suffered. The gap between the ecstasy of heaven and the pain of earth was never wider than on the cross. Jesus understands the experience of a painful world.

Jesus also reveals why we should trust his authority. *Jesus affirms the True Self of the Seven by celebrating and enjoying parties.* There is no way to read the Gospels without noticing that Jesus *really* enjoyed celebrating.

LIKE THE SEVEN, JESUS LOST TRUE PARADISE AND EXPERIENCED A PAINFUL WORLD.

His first miracle was turning water into wine. (And we're told he made the best wine!) He loved sharing a good meal with people from all walks of life. He enjoyed celebrating so much that he was

falsely accused of being a drunkard and a glutton (Matthew 11:19). Kids seemed to flock to him—surely a testament to his playfulness. Unlike the stoic, flat, and, dare I say, *boring* depictions of Jesus we often see, Jesus was

LIKE THE SEVEN, JESUS ENJOYED PARTIES AND CELEBRATING.

vivacious, charismatic, and full of life.

Like the Seven, Jesus was curious about people. Over the years of conducting interviews for two podcasts, I've learned that asking a *good* question can lead to fascinating places. The healthy Seven does this naturally, and so did Jesus. He would routinely ask questions to explore the minds, hearts, and experiences of the people around him. He was curious about what motivated people and what they wanted out of their lives. He brilliantly answered questions by posing new questions—thereby allowing what was hidden inside other people to become exposed. Jesus' curiosity was contagious. People often left conversations with Jesus with a greater sense of curiosity about themselves, about life, and about God.

However, Jesus confronts the False Self of the Seven by enduring suffering to obtain true joy. Jesus' joy was not a hedonistic joy built on

avoidance of pain. Nor did Jesus view suffering as meaningless. He understood that suffering is an essential part of the process that brings us life. About Jesus, Hebrews 12:2 says, "For the joy set before him he endured the cross." When we make our own

JESUS CONFRONTS THE SEVEN BY ENDURING SUFFERING TO OBTAIN TRUE JOY.

personal happiness the highest good, we make ourselves our own reason for living. When we pursue the flourishing of others as the highest good, we find a reason for life that gives purpose to suffering. Jesus shows us that by being selfless, suffering becomes meaningful.[8]

Also, Jesus valued people more than experiences. In Matthew 6:25, Jesus says, "Therefore I tell you, do not worry about your life, what you will eat or drink; or about your body, what you will wear. Is not life more than food, and the body more than clothes?" Jesus did not mistake the pleasure of indulgence for life itself. When the temple guards came to arrest Jesus, Peter attacked them in an attempt to protect Jesus (John 18:10). Jesus reminded everyone present that he could call down legions of angels to defend him if he wanted (Matthew 26:53). He could have chosen a less painful, easier, and more enjoyable life for himself. Instead he chose to love others. The apostle Paul writes, "For you know the grace of our Lord Jesus Christ, that though he was rich, yet for your sake he became poor, so that you through his poverty might become rich" (2 Corinthians 8:9). Jesus did not use people for the sake of what he preferred; he sacrificed what he preferred for the sake of people.

How did Jesus display joy and celebration without ever succumbing to the deadly sin of gluttony? Why didn't Jesus believe he needed constant pleasure? *Jesus believed he would be taken care of.* In Gethsemane, Jesus was hours away from the cross, where he would take on himself all the sins of history. In this moment of anguish, Jesus prayed, "Father, if you are willing, take this cup from me; yet not my will, but yours be done" (Luke 22:42). Though an angel came to strengthen him, his pain was not taken away, nor was the burden of the cross removed. God cared for Jesus by giving him the strength to endure and the faith to trust that true joy was on the other side of his suffering. That level of trust and surrender is astounding. It's delayed gratification on a cosmic scale.

Redeeming Your True Self: From Avoidance to Substance

**THE SEVEN IS GIVEN THE GOOD NEWS,
"I WILL TAKE CARE OF YOU."**

The Seven needs someone to find them in their greatest moment of fear and anxiety, someone who will see their needs and tend to them. God meets the Seven, stoops low, and sees them. He knows about their fear of being trapped in pain, their loss of paradise, and their worship of indulgence and gluttony. He meets them in their anxiety, their pain, and their worries and takes the hand of the child inside. To the Seven, God says, *"I will take care of you."* The Seven finds in the gospel the very thing they are looking for—to be truly happy.

In Matthew 6:8, Jesus says, "Your Father knows what you need before you ask him." Later, he tells his disciples, "Are not two sparrows sold for a penny? Yet not one of them will fall to the ground outside your Father's care. And even the very hairs of your head are all numbered. So don't be afraid; you are worth more than many sparrows" (Matthew 10:29–31). God relieves us of the burden to always care for our own needs.

However, the Scriptures do not promise that God will relieve us of our pain in this life. The Bible makes it clear that we should anticipate troubles and hardships (John 16:33). Jesus wasn't immune. The disciples weren't either. Neither are we. How is God meeting our needs, we may be asking, if we continue to suffer?

Let's ask ourselves, *What is true happiness?* The Bible calls it joy. It's stronger, deeper, and more enduring than our world's idea of happiness. If this world is the only life we have, then when suffering or trouble comes and steals our happiness, we may lose happiness forever. If that is true, we would be right to despair and put ourselves and our appetites first. But if this world is not all there is, if

Jesus truly does love us, if he really did defeat sin and conquer the power of death, and if we are destined for a climactic future in which every tear is wiped away and pain is no more (Revelation 21:3–4), then we can join the apostle Paul in saying, "I consider that our present sufferings are not worth comparing with the glory that will be revealed in us" (Romans 8:18). While shallow happiness is destroyed by circumstances, joy endures. God meets our needs by giving us a happiness that can never be extinguished.

Unlike shallow happiness, which fades as we age, joy burns brighter with every passing year. God does not promise to give us new circumstances, but he does promise to give us new character. He meets our needs by forging our character and enabling us to find joy in every circumstance. This is true happiness.

What if the Seven were to allow God's ever-present care to fill their heart and imagination? What if the Holy Spirit plants the hope and joy of Christ deeper and deeper into the life of the Seven? What would it look like to entrust their life, character, and personality to Jesus? It would look like *surrender*. Psychologist David Benner writes, "Far from being a sign of weakness, only surrender to something or someone bigger than us is sufficiently strong to free us from the prison of our egocentricity. Only surrender is powerful enough to overcome our isolation and alienation."[9] What does surrender look like?

First, it helps to take an inventory of how gluttony has harmed our life. When we confess that we have put our hope in gluttony to fix our problems, refused to admit gluttony was wrong, and blamed others while insisting they cater to our desires, small but important shifts in our heart begin to happen. Gluttony loses its power over us. We must take gluttony off the throne so we can be filled and formed by the power of God.

Second, to counteract their gluttony, the Seven will want to practice the virtue of *sobriety*.[10] The apostle Peter tells us, "Be sober-minded; be watchful. Your adversary the devil prowls around like

TO COMBAT GLUTTONY, PRACTICE SOBRIETY.

BE LEVELHEADED AND LIVE IN THE REALITY OF THE MOMENT WITHOUT SEEKING DISTRACTIONS.

a roaring lion, seeking someone to devour" (1 Peter 5:8 ESV). Sobriety is about living in the reality of the current moment just as it is. We accept that both pleasure and pain are part of life and that there is no need to look over the horizon for a way to escape. We learn to take only what we need—no more, no less—because no amount of excess can satisfy what our soul truly wants. Sobriety isn't just about no longer gorging ourselves on food, gambling, or partying, but about allowing ourselves to experience more stillness. It's hard to hear God's voice when we're always blasting the stereo in our minds.

As we trust God's grace to care for our sin and our fears, we find the courage to get in touch with the dark parts of ourselves. Sobriety allows us to entrust our wounds and fears to God, to explore the reasons we've been indulging, and to grieve the impact it has had on our lives.

My friend Jonah is a Seven.[11] After years of suffering under gluttony with a food addiction, his weight had grown to nearly double the ideal weight for his height. After seeking out a spiritual mentor for help, he eventually recognized that his thoughts were lying to him. He realized that he ate because he felt alone, out of control, and overwhelmed. He told me, "All my thoughts of 'If I only had more' were killing me. Not only was the shame and fear killing me, but these things were also *actually* going to kill me."

Sitting in solitude, he began to unravel the lies he was telling himself and found the courage to surrender to God by pursuing sobriety. He said, "It's the natural rhythms of repentance. You see something that's lying to you, and you turn to God. In the presence of God, you ask, *Why am I so scared? What am I scared about? Reveal to me what's really going on. Show me the hard things I don't want to see.*

And that's really hard for Sevens. To do that, I need to believe God is going to care for me."

In time, transformation happened. By allowing God to tend to his emotional wounds, Jonah found the courage to practice sobriety. Not only did he begin to experience more relational intimacy with God and others, but he was also able to achieve a healthier weight.

When the Seven practices sobriety, their life begins to grow a variety of good fruit. *First, practicing sobriety allows the Seven to experience true joy.* Fake joy is about avoidance. True joy is about substance. As the Seven follows Jesus, true joy emerges—because to know Jesus is to know joy.[12]

Second, they become more grounded. Like the string of a kite being held by a child, sobriety tethers the Seven to the ground. Instead of filling their time with habitual daydreaming and future planning, the disciplined Seven practices being in the moment and attentive to those around them. They learn to have reasonable expectations and how to care for their life as it is today.

Third, they develop perseverance. The apostle Paul writes, "We rejoice in our sufferings, knowing that suffering produces endurance, and endurance produces character, and character produces hope" (Romans 5:3–4 ESV). These attributes only develop if the Seven remains sober amid their suffering. Developing this character gives the Seven the pleasure of putting action behind their ideas in order to finish what they start. They can focus on what matters and become people whose commitments are trustworthy.

Discipleship: Feasting and Silence and Solitude

To keep themselves from falling back into gluttony and indulgence, the Seven will want to walk with Jesus through two specific spiritual disciplines.[13] *The first spiritual discipline the Seven should practice is feasting.* Just as Jesus enjoyed food and fellowship, the Seven will benefit from doing the same. Use this time to cultivate relationships, have meaningful conversations, and pray for those present. However, the Seven should avoid both excess and escapism. This is not a time to binge, nor is it a time to avoid our inner world. If we do these things, we are not practicing the discipline but merely masking our gluttony behind Christian language.

The other discipline the Seven should practice is daily silence and solitude. Being alone away from people and screens will allow the Seven to quiet their inner chatter and flurry of activity. This is the space where the Seven is most likely to notice their own inner life and also hear from God. One Seven I know walked the same two-mile trail every day for a year. During this time, he would pray and take notice of his own thoughts and emotions. The result was a man who was still fun and exciting to be with while being more emotionally attuned, wise, and grounded.

The False Self will not go away easily. We should be aware of the fact that it often works like a river. When we dam up one path, it will often create a new one. As the Seven walks with Jesus in sobriety and truth, they will be shaped more and more into the likeness of their teacher. Change may be slow, but it is inevitable.

THE SEVEN REFLECTS GOD'S JOY & ABUNDANCE.

Each of the traits of the Enneagram—when healthy—reflect a different aspect of God's character. *The True Self of the Seven reflects God's joy and abundance.*[14] Jesus tells us that if we follow in his lifestyle, we will abide in his love and that our joy will be full (John 15:9–11). When the Seven follows Jesus and receives from him, their joy helps the world understand the celebration and vivaciousness of Jesus himself. The world sees hope for their pain. When the Seven learns how to be satisfied by God's care, they help the world wake up from its trance and see the abundance of God that is already here and available to us. They show the world that the kingdom of God is a party!

Practical Tips for the Seven

1. Be mindful of your numbing strategies. What self-medicating tactics do you use when you're feeling bored, scared, or angry? Write them down.

2. Build structure into your day in order to stay on task. Make to-do lists and deadlines for yourself. Stay focused by keeping them in regular view.

3. Know the difference between wants and needs. When we mistake wants for needs, we slip into a spirit of entitlement. Do you *need* it or just *want* it?

4. Schedule margin and protect it. Don't fill your schedule with nonstop activity and entertainment. Practice reflective silence and solitude.

5. Learn to listen to others or you'll be ignored. If you overtake every conversation, people will feel unheard and will stop listening to you.

6. Volunteer your time regularly. To get outside of yourself, simply be present for those in pain. Try to compassionately empathize with their hardships.

CONCLUSION

A New Way to Relate

The Enneagram helps us to see the way we relate, but Jesus transforms the way we relate.

No one who encounters Jesus ever stays the same. I'm not referring to a Jesus you create or that you project your desires onto. That isn't Jesus; it's just your type dressed up as God. That Jesus doesn't contradict you or challenge you or help you. If you're going to experience true transformation, you must encounter "the real Jesus."[1]

In Jesus, we find more than our one-dimensional type; we find the most dynamic man who ever lived.

Jesus is:

The True Reformer
The True Helper
The True Achiever
The True Originalist
The True Investigator
The True Loyalist

The True Enthusiast

The True Protector

The True Peacemaker

Though Jesus expresses the gifts of our type with purity, he is not merely a type. He is all the types and more. He has no False Self, no dark side, no twisted adaptations. He is the unblemished fullness of God and humanity. He is both our Savior and our Exemplar, sent by the Father for our sake.

Author Neal Lozano writes, "The Father's heart is broken for you. He sent his Son to reveal His love and do whatever it takes to win back your heart. He longs to bring you home. Jesus endured the cross for the joy set before Him; it was the joy of finding you. You are the one lost sheep, the penny, the son from Jesus' parables. Jesus left heaven to search after you."[2]

WHERE IS CHRIST IN THE ENNEAGRAM?

CHRIST CAME TO REVEAL AND PUT TO DEATH OUR FALSE SELF AND RECLAIM OUR TRUE SELF.

Jesus wants to give us life to the fullest, to set us free from our False Self, to engulf us in his love so we may freely love others. Jesus wants to make dead people dance, prisoners whoop for joy in the streets, and the poor feel like they've won the lottery. Jesus has come to set you free.

However, to truly believe this, you have to trust him. Has he earned your trust?

Trusting Jesus with Your Whole Self

We have trusted our idols and our deadly sins to save us. They have failed. They've made our life worse instead of better. To change our allegiances, we must transfer our trust.

As we said before, for someone to earn the right to guide us on major decisions in life, they must do two things: empathize with us and display their authority. If someone only empathizes with us, we find a listening ear but no proven path forward. If someone only models their authority, we find a solution

EMPATHY + AUTHORITY = TRUST

ONLY JESUS HAS THE EMPATHY AND AUTHORITY TO DESERVE OUR TOTAL TRUST.

but no love. When we believe someone understands our pain from firsthand experience and has demonstrated their authority about how to live life to the fullest, they will earn our trust and the right to guide us. (Empathy + Authority = Trust.)

As we have seen throughout our investigation into all nine types, Jesus both empathizes with our pain and proves his expertise on life and relationships. No one wants better for us than Jesus does. Who loves you more than Jesus? He alone is worthy of your complete trust.

In Jesus we can look at ourselves for who we *really* are. Only through Jesus can we look at reality without having it crush us.

Redemption of our True Selves happens in two primary ways: God heals our wounds and calls us to change the way we live. If we receive healing without repentance, we end up using God for our own gain—like the nine lepers who were healed by Jesus, never to return to him (Luke 17:11–19). If we repent without being healed, we become legalistic. We have simply directed our wounds down a new path.

As James Cofield once told me, "We need to be *healed* from the sins done to us. We need to *repent* of the sin we do to others." Both healing and repenting are key elements of new life. What, then, is the source for both?

The Gospel of Delight, Presence, and Grace

As we have explored throughout this book, our False Self is driven by our fear, guilt, and shame. We are afraid we will be hurt. We are culpable for our bad behavior. We are humiliated by our flaws. These three underlying realities have deformed our soul and our relationships. How can this disease in our soul be healed? God provides the antidote to this poison:

> *God heals our guilt with his grace.*
> *God heals our shame with his delight.*
> *God heals our fear with his presence.*

Many explorations of the gospel emphasize our guilt before a holy God and his atonement for our sins on the cross. The Scriptures teach in Romans 6:23, "The wages of sin is death, but the gift of God is eternal life in Christ Jesus our Lord." Jesus sacrificed himself for our sake. Through Jesus' blood on the cross, our sinful state is replaced with his perfect holiness. We receive his goodness in place of our guilt. This is the gospel of grace. What profoundly good news!

And yet we must remember it's not the full picture. Though our guilt is addressed, our shame and fear often remain unhealed. We must also understand that God's presence and delight are essential to our healing. A child who has been forgiven and yet still feels abandoned and insecure is hardly a child who has experienced good news.

In Zephaniah 3:17, we see God's delight, presence, and grace converge in a single image:

> The LORD your God is with you,
>> the Mighty Warrior who saves.
> He will take great delight in you;
>> in his love he will no longer rebuke you,
>> but will rejoice over you with singing.

God is *with you* (presence); he will take great *delight in you* (delight); he will *no longer rebuke you, but will rejoice over you* (grace).

Remember, the Triads reveal our existential questions in life. The Heart Triad asks, *Who am I?* The Head Triad asks, *Where am I?* The Body Triad asks, *How am I doing?* It is in the gospel that we finally find the answers to our existential questions:

TO STOP RELYING ON OUR PERSONALITY TO SAVE US, WE MUST LET JESUS SAVE US.

POISON	ANTIDOTE
SHAME →	DELIGHT
FEAR →	PRESENCE
GUILT →	GRACE

Who am I? I am a child in whom God delights.
Where am I? I am secure in the presence of God.
How am I doing? I am free in the grace of God.

This is the wellspring from which we live.

Brennan Manning once wrote, "If you took the love of all the best mothers and fathers who have lived in the course of human history, all their goodness, kindness, patience, fidelity, wisdom, tenderness, strength, and love and united all those qualities in a single person, that person's love would only be a faint shadow of the furious love and mercy in the heart of God the Father addressed to you and me at this moment."[3] We do not decide whether we are worthy of God's love. In words attributed to Saint Augustine, "In loving me, you made me lovable."[4]

Are you a sinner? Yes. However, many of you believe the deepest thing about you is that you are a sinner. That is not true. The deepest thing about you is that you are loved.

If you believe that, then a new way of relating can finally emerge.

The Enneagram Types as the Body of Christ

The apostle Paul writes, "Just as each of us has one body with many members, and these members do not all have the same function, so in Christ we, though many, form one body, and each member belongs to all the others" (Romans 12:4–5). To live in the fullness of life, we need one another. We are each coals in a fire, burning brighter because of the heat of the others. Take us away from one another, and we grow dim and cold.

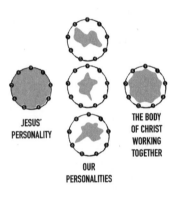

JESUS' PERSONALITY

OUR PERSONALITIES

THE BODY OF CHRIST WORKING TOGETHER

We have said that Jesus was the full embodiment of all nine types. He manifested the very best of each of the traits. When we stand alone, we are a dim and cold reflection of who he was. However, when we come together in a beloved community, we begin to reveal a clearer picture of Jesus to the world.

The One ensures the church reflects the righteousness and integrity of Jesus.

The Two ensures the church reflects the servanthood and compassion of Jesus.

The Three ensures the church reflects the vision and ambition of Jesus.

The Four ensures the church reflects the sensitivity and creativity of Jesus.

The Five ensures the church reflects the wisdom and contemplation of Jesus.

The Six ensures the church reflects the covenant and reliability of Jesus.

The Seven ensures the church reflects the joy and celebration of Jesus.

The Eight ensures the church reflects the protection and clarity of Jesus.

The Nine ensures the church reflects the peace and
acceptance of Jesus.

In the church, when we show favoritism to one type over the others, we end up championing just one personality rather than the full image of Jesus. In order for the world to see Jesus, we must come together and value all the types and every member of the body. We're at our best when we're all together.

As Dr. Tony Evans once said, "Unity is not uniformity; unity is oneness of purpose . . . An orchestra is unified not because all the instruments are the same, but because the different instruments are playing the same song."[5] This is why the Scriptures call us to unity. Ephesians 4:3 reads, "Make every effort to keep the unity of the Spirit through the bond of peace."

TOGETHER, WE REFLECT JESUS TO THE WORLD.

We cannot live as our True Selves apart from relationships. We need Jesus, and we need one another.

We must live in unity with one another to reflect Christ to the world.

Final Thoughts

John Calvin once declared, "Nearly all the wisdom we possess, that is to say, true and sound wisdom, consists of two parts: the knowledge of God and of ourselves."[6] To truly know ourselves is to be encouraged and humbled, affirmed and confronted. Self-clarity drives us into the arms of God because we see our deep need for him. As the Enneagram has shown us, our insides are a bundle of Christmas lights—beautiful yet tied into so many knots we have no hope of fixing it ourselves. And yet we find ourselves in the most trustworthy hands possible.

We began our journey together in the same place we should now end: God's great desire is for you to love and be loved in relationships.

Though our sin and our wounds have diminished our relationships, Jesus is intent on restoring them. He came to give you the freedom, security, and identity your soul has searched for. He has spared you from using your gifts in unhealthy ways in relationships. You no longer need to manipulate people to get affirmation, to scheme to feel secure, or to overreact to a hostile world. He showers you with his delight, comforts you with his presence, and emboldens you with his grace. Your life is meaningful because your relationships are meaningful.

The world desperately needs people who are good at relationships. Why? Because the purpose of life is relationships. The world will know we are Christians by how we relate. Let's go build better relationships.

WINGS

Much like someone will customize their coffee with their favorite creamer, people customize their *core type* utilizing one of their wings. Wings are the numbers on each side of your core type. Typically, one wing influences your core type more than the other. However, it is also possible to have both wings be a significant influence or to have neither wing exert much influence. As you read the table below, consider whether you sense the presence of one wing, no wings, or both wings in your personality.

THE HEART TRIAD		
TYPE	WING	WING
Two	One: Tend to be more idealistic, objective, self-critical, and judgmental.	Three: Tend to be more self-assured, ambitious, outgoing, and competitive.
Three	Two: Tend to be warmer, more encouraging, sociable, popular, and alluring.	Four: Tend to be more introspective, sensitive, artistic, imaginative, and pretentious.
Four	Three: Tend to be more extroverted, upbeat, ambitious, attention-seeking, and image-conscious.	Five: Tend to be more introverted, intellectual, atypical, reserved, and depressed.

THE HEAD TRIAD		
TYPE	WING	WING
Five	Four: Tend to be more creative, focused on human welfare, sensitive, empathetic, and self-absorbed.	Six: Tend to be more loyal, anxious, skeptical, cautious, and interested in research and science.
Six	Five: Tend to be more introverted, intellectual, cautious, and distant.	Seven: Tend to be more extroverted, materialistic, active, and impulsive.
Seven	Six: Tend to be more loyal, endearing, responsible, and anxious.	Eight: Tend to be more energetic, aggressive, competitive, and materialistic.
THE BODY TRIAD		
TYPE	WING	WING
Eight	Seven: Tend to be more extroverted, enterprising, energetic, quick, and self-centered.	Nine: Tend to be more mild-mannered, gentle, receptive, and quietly strong.
Nine	Eight: Tend to be more outgoing, assertive, anti-authoritarian, and prone to switch between being confrontational and conciliatory.	One: Tend to be more orderly, critical, emotionally controlled, and compliant.
One	Nine: Tend to be cooler, more relaxed, objective, and detached.	Two: Tend to be warmer, more helpful, critical, and controlling.

ARROWS

•————————•

Each type also connects with two additional types in the circle. You connect with one type under stressful conditions and one under secure conditions. In both cases, when you're in an unhealthy place, you will tend to take on the nonresourceful aspects of those types. When you're in a healthy space, you're likely to take on the resourceful aspects of both types. When this is happening, you don't change types; rather, you simply display characteristics from that type. Find your type below to learn more.

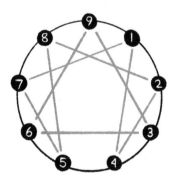

THE HEART TRIAD

TYPE	STRESS ARROW	SECURE ARROW
Two	**Eight:** Can be irritable and attack others, can blame, make demands and attempt to control everyone *or* feel more self-confident and straightforward, will feel less concerned with other's opinions of them.	**Four:** Can accept their painful feelings including sadness and anger, explore their inner world and utilize boundaries *or* get trapped in comparing their life to others and become self-absorbed in sadness.
Three	**Nine:** Can become indecisive, procrastinating and apathetic, can numb out and avoid responsibility *or* can slow down and relax, become more receptive and see life with a broader view.	**Six:** Can spend more intentional time with friends and family and put the needs of the group first, can get in touch with their feelings *or* become afraid of rejection, become more anxious and have trouble making decisions.
Four	**Two:** Can become manipulative to get affection, can exaggerate their pain for attention, can deny their needs *or* can connect with people deeply, focus on others more, serve others unconditionally.	**One:** Can be more self-disciplined and do more problem solving, more easily expresses gratitude and is less controlled by their feelings *or* can be critical and unappeasable, can be excessively moral and feel buried in guilt.

THE HEAD TRIAD

TYPE	STRESS ARROW	SECURE ARROW
Five	**Seven:** Can take on new projects impulsively, become scattered, numb their anxiety through harmful self-medicating *or* become less self-conscious, become more fun-loving and openly celebratory.	**Eight:** Can get in touch with their body and put their thoughts into action, become more outspoken and assertive *or* become punitive and unreasonable, openly ignore other people's feelings and desires.

Six	Three: Can try to avoid their anxiety by staying busy, resist anything new where they may fail, overidentify with their image and lie to succeed *or* take decisive and effective action and feel good about their accomplishments.	Nine: Can be more empathetic, have a broader perspective, relax to free up their energy and trust themselves more *or* numb themselves through excessive self-medicating, become apathetic.
Seven	One: Can become cynical, judgmental and hypercritical; be certain that they "know" the truth more than others, blame others *or* become more productive and complete what they start, become less self-centered and focus on the needs of others.	Five: Can become quieter and more introspective, explore subjects in more depth, can become more serious and be taken more seriously *or* push their theories onto others and become more self-absorbed and avoid responsibilities.

THE BODY TRIAD

TYPE	STRESS ARROW	SECURE ARROW
Eight	Five: Can withdraw from others and their own feelings, become paranoid about being controlled, and become depressed *or* become more objective, think things through before acting, and learn to control their impulses.	Two: Can become more emotionally vulnerable and more concerned for the welfare of others, become more loving and lovable *or* become more defensive and overreactive, unrealistic in their demands and codependent.
Nine	Six: Can become overwhelmed by anxiety, indecisive, rigid and self-doubting, inactive and passive *or* become more direct and outspoken, more loyal and realistic.	Three: Can become more energetic, productive, focused, self-directed and self-confident *or* take on more than they can handle, try to impress people by meeting the goals of others instead of their own.
One	Four: Can be indignant or depressed when expectations aren't met, can feel unlovable *or* they can get in touch with deeper feelings and get involved in creative activities.	Seven: Can be less critical and self-accepting, can be celebratory and optimistic *or* they can become self-destructive through excessive behaviors and substance abuse.

ACKNOWLEDGMENTS

———•———

I am indebted to the many Enneagram teachers and authors whose work contributed to themes in this book. Though I sometimes deviated significantly from their original language or conclusions, I want to credit a few teachers for concepts I drew on heavily.

True Self and False Self: Richard Plass and James Cofield (*The Relational Soul: Moving from False Self to Deep Connection*)

Childhood and Adolescence: Don Richard Riso and Russ Hudson (*The Wisdom of the Enneagram: The Complete Guide to Psychological and Spiritual Growth for the Nine Personality Types*)

Idols: Jerome Wagner ("From Idolatry to Reality: From Worshiping the Idealizations of Our Personality to Following the Ideals of Our Real Self")

The Deadly Sins: Don Richard Riso and Russ Hudson (*The Wisdom of the Enneagram*)

The Enneagram Traits in Jesus: Richard Rohr and Andreas Ebert (*The Enneagram: A Christian Perspective*); Robert J. Nogosek (*Nine Portraits of Jesus: Discovering Jesus through the Enneagram*)

How Jesus Confronts Each Type: Clarence Thomson (*Parables and the Enneagram*)

The Good News for Each Type: Beth McCord and Jeff McCord (*Becoming Us: Using the Enneagram to Create a Thriving Gospel-Centered Marriage*)

The Virtues: Don Richard Riso and Russ Hudson (*The Wisdom of the Enneagram*)

The Spiritual Disciplines for Each Type: AJ Sherrill (*The Enneagram for Spiritual Formation: How Knowing Ourselves Can Make Us More Like Jesus*)

How Each Type Reflects God: Marilyn Vancil (*Self to Lose, Self to Find: Using the Enneagram to Discover Your True, God-Gifted Self*)

Additional influences include Ian Morgan Cron, Suzanne Stabile, Beatrice Chestnut, Renee Baron, Elizabeth Wagele, and Sarajane Case.

Though his book *Building a StoryBrand* is not specifically Enneagram-based, Donald Miller makes excellent observations about how empathy and authority lead to trust.

· • ● ● ● ● · ·

And now, a variety of gratitude is in order:

Thank you to the Love Thy Neighborhood staff whose faithfulness and care allowed me to write this book: Rachel Szabo, Anna Tran, Rachel Hamm, Kirsten Cragg, Anna Johnson, Lauren Maddux, Samuel Thomas, Marley McCune, and Leandro Lozada. Thank you to my *EnneaCast* cohosts Lindsey Lewis and Sam Stevenson. Endless, eternal thanks to my ministry partner-in-crime, Kiana Brown, for serving us all with more sweat and care than what is fair or reasonable. May you get all the house plants you could ever want.

Thank you to the Love Thy Neighborhood board for supporting this book from start to finish: Mark Minnery, Jonathan Butler, Kim Blinkhorn, Bill Nunnery, Hong Sui, Chanda Hand, Michael Hall, Dave Burnette, Hilary Noltemeyer, and Jesse Faught. Extra gratitude to Brent Walker for interning with me as I began writing. Your attentive presence made such a difference.

Thank you to Jennifer Nickel for coaching me through my insecurities and cheering me onward. Thank you to Mike Cosper for listening to my scattered ideas and opening the door for me. Without both of you encouraging me, I would have kept this boat tied up at shore.

Thank you to my agent, Don Gates. This book was only a dream until you came along. Thank you to the innovative and amazing team at Zondervan: Meaghan Minkus, Dirk Buursma, Paul Fisher, Devin Duke, Matt Bray, and Katie Painter. Deepest thanks to Andy Rogers for seeing my vision and taking a chance on this project.

Thank you to all the people who generously gave me places to hide away and write: Kyle and Hilary Noltemeyer, Mary and Dan Parker, Caroline and Lorne Belding, David and Wendy Novak, and Jonathan and Ashley Butler. A quiet place of solitude is a gift.

Thank you far and wide to the following: Sojourn Church Midtown, Jamaal and Amber Williams, Alex and LB O'Nan, Coury and Anne Deeb, Michael and Kimiko Muwanguzi, Simon Groce, Reid Olson, Lachlan Coffee, Ben Mast, Skye Jethani, Jeff and Beth McCord, Lisa Vischer, Janet Price, Carson-Meyer Foundation, Bonnie Epperson, and Southeast Christian Church.

Thank you to Rich Plass and Jim Cofield for training me in the Enneagram. Thank you for your courageous generosity and for lighting the way on this beautiful but disorienting path. Your investment in people will ripple through generations.

Thank you to my family: Lee-Anne, Joel, Nate, Norah, Naomi, Carol, Bill, Reva, and Dad. Mom—I miss you.

Thank you to my children, Evangeline and Justus. In all of my wildest type 4 fantasies, I could never have dreamt big enough to imagine either of you. It is the greatest honor of my life to be your father. Your existence fills me with delight. Finally, thank you to Lindsay My Beautiful. Your empathy, encouragement, and sacrifice made this book possible. What a fun addition to the story we've been writing together. Seasons change, but some things will remain. You are God's gift to me.

NOTES

Introduction

1. See Paul Akin, "The Number One Reason Missionaries Go Home," Gospel Coalition, June 15, 2017, www.thegospelcoalition .org/article/the-number-one-reason-missionaries-go-home.
2. Richard Rohr, *Things Hidden: Scripture as Spirituality* (Cincinnati, OH: Franciscan Media, 2008), 56–57.
3. See CrossPoint Ministry, *The Relational Enneagram Workbook* (Louisville, KY: CrossPoint Ministry, 2021), 10.
4. See AJ Sherrill, *The Enneagram for Spiritual Formation: How Knowing Ourselves Can Make Us More Like Jesus* (Grand Rapids: Brazos, 2020), 13.
5. If you have concerns or questions about the Enneagram, see Tyler Zach, "Should Christians Use the Enneagram?" Gospel Coalition, November 16, 2020, https://gcdiscipleship.com/article-feed/should -christians-use-the-enneagram. See also a similar article with the same title (Tyler Zach, "Should Christians Use the Enneagram?" Gospel for Enneagram, July 23, 2020, https://gospelforenneagram .com/christian-enneagram.
6. Timothy Keller, Twitter post, May 2, 2019, 6:23 a.m., https:// twitter.com/timkellernyc/status/1123895657008369667?lang=en.

Chapter 1: Created for Community

1. Richard Plass and James Cofield, *The Relational Soul: Moving from False Self to Deep Connection* (Downers Grove, IL: InterVarsity, 2014), 13.
2. I am indebted to Richard Plass and James Cofield for both their book *The Relational Soul* and their work on the Enneagram, which has only been partially published. This chapter is deeply informed by their teaching. You can visit www.crosspointministry.com to learn about their work and their approach to the Enneagram.
3. As C. S. Lewis once wrote, "The doors of hell are locked on the *inside*" (*The Problem of Pain* [New York: Macmillan, 1962], 127, italics in original).

4. Again, I am indebted to Richard Plass and James Cofield for this insightful term. "Expressed Self" serves as a missing link connecting the concepts of the True Self, False Self, and Personality.

5. See John 13:34–35.

Chapter 2: The Enneagram

1. Harper Lee, *To Kill a Mockingbird* (New York: Grand Central, 1960), 39.

2. In his book *The Dynamic Heart in Daily Life: Connecting Christ to Human Experience* (Greensboro, NC: New Growth, 2016), Jeremy Pierre explores this idea in more depth than I have space for here. He says, "Scripture uses different anthropological terms—heart, soul, spirit, mind, and more—to describe a simple, singular human experience" (p. 26).

3. See CrossPoint Ministry, *The Relational Enneagram Workbook* (Louisville, KY: CrossPoint Ministry, 2021); Jerome Wagner, *Nine Lenses on the World: The Enneagram Perspective* (Evanston, IL: NineLens, 2010), 142.

Chapter 3: Type Eight

1. See Don Richard Riso and Russ Hudson, *The Wisdom of the Enneagram: The Complete Guide to Psychological and Spiritual Growth for the Nine Personality Types* (New York: Bantam, 1999), 31.

2. See Riso and Hudson, *Wisdom of the Enneagram*, 32.

3. CrossPoint Ministry, *The Relational Enneagram Workbook* (Louisville, KY: CrossPoint Ministry, 2021), 44.

4. See Riso and Hudson, *Wisdom of the Enneagram*, 34.

5. See Riso and Hudson, *Wisdom of the Enneagram*, 33.

6. See Jerome Wagner, "From Idolatry to Reality: From Worshiping the Idealizations of Our Personality to Following the Ideals of Our Real Self," The Enneagram Spectrum of Personality Styles, accessed June 14, 2022, http://enneagramspectrum.com/1293 /from-idolatry-to-reality.

7. Philip Yancey, *Disappointment with God: Three Questions No One Asks Aloud* (Grand Rapids: Zondervan, 2015), 71.

8. Traditionally, the deadly sin for the Eight is *lust*. However, the tendency to understand lust with a purely sexual connotation

renders that word misleading. Boundlessness can certainly influence sexuality, but it is not exclusively sexual.

9. William Gurnall, *The Christian in Complete Armour* (1655; repr., London: Tegg, 1862), 100.

10. Jerome Wagner, *Nine Lenses on the World: The Enneagram Perspective* (Evanston, IL: NineLens, 2010), 54.

11. Catherine Booth, *For God Alone* (Belfast, UK: Emerald House, 1990), 158.

12. Scott Sauls, "Damaged Humans and the Kindness of God," March 18, 2022, https://scottsauls.com/blog/2022/03/18/damaged.

13. Listen to the *BEMA Discipleship Podcast* ("Season 3, Session 76: Silent Years—Sadducees," June 7, 2018, www.bemadiscipleship .com/76) for an in-depth exploration of what I refer to here. In fact, I recommend listening to the entire "Silent Years" series (Season 3, Sessions 73–81, www.bemadiscipleship.com/episodes /page/1?season=3) for more cultural context for Jesus' ministry. There's a whole lot of drama hidden in the text we often miss.

14. Philip Yancey, *The Jesus I Never Knew* (Grand Rapids: Zondervan, 1995), 80, italics in original.

15. Dane Ortlund, *Gentle and Lowly: The Heart of Christ for Sinners and Sufferers* (Wheaton, IL: Crossway, 2020), 198.

16. See Wagner, *Nine Lenses on the World*, 84.

17. Gretel Ehrlich, *The Solace of Open Spaces* (New York: Penguin, 1986), 44.

18. See AJ Sherrill, *The Enneagram for Spiritual Formation: How Knowing Ourselves Can Make Us More Like Jesus* (Grand Rapids: Brazos, 2020), 78.

19. See Marilyn Vancil, *Self to Lose, Self to Find: Using the Enneagram to Discover Your True, God-Gifted Self* (New York: Convergent, 2020), 121.

Chapter 4: Type Nine

1. Don Richard Riso and Russ Hudson, *The Wisdom of the Enneagram: The Complete Guide to Psychological and Spiritual Growth for the Nine Personality Types* (New York: Bantam, 1999), 317.

2. See Riso and Hudson, *Wisdom of the Enneagram*, 31.

3. See Riso and Hudson, *Wisdom of the Enneagram*, 32.

4. See CrossPoint Ministry, *The Relational Enneagram Workbook* (Louisville, KY: CrossPoint Ministry, 2021), 48.

5. See Riso and Hudson, *Wisdom of the Enneagram*, 34.

6. See Riso and Hudson, *Wisdom of the Enneagram*, 33.

7. Mike Birbiglia, *Sleepwalk with Me and Other Painfully True Stories* (New York: Simon & Schuster, 2010), 141.

8. Clarence Thomson, *Parables and the Enneagram* (Portland, OR: Metamorphous, 1996), 131.

9. See Jerome Wagner, *Nine Lenses on the World: The Enneagram Perspective* (Evanston, IL: NineLens, 2010), 54.

10. Marilyn Vancil, *Self to Lose, Self to Find: Using the Enneagram to Discover Your True, God-Gifted Self* (New York: Convergent, 2020), 131.

11. AJ Sherrill, *The Enneagram for Spiritual Formation: How Knowing Ourselves Can Make Us More Like Jesus* (Grand Rapids: Brazos, 2020), 79.

12. See Vancil, *Self to Lose, Self to Find*, 130.

Chapter 5: Type One

1. See Don Richard Riso and Russ Hudson, *The Wisdom of the Enneagram: The Complete Guide to Psychological and Spiritual Growth for the Nine Personality Types* (New York: Bantam, 1999), 31.

2. Riso and Hudson, *Wisdom of the Enneagram*, 32.

3. CrossPoint Ministry, *The Relational Enneagram Workbook* (Louisville, KY: CrossPoint Ministry, 2021), 52.

4. See Riso and Hudson, *Wisdom of the Enneagram*, 34.

5. See Riso and Hudson, *Wisdom of the Enneagram*, 33.

6. Donald Miller, *Scary Close: Dropping the Act and Finding True Intimacy* (Nashville: Nelson, 2014), 65.

7. The traditional vice for the One is *anger*, but I find this to be too broad. (Also, anger is not exclusively a negative emotion.) More specifically, CrossPoint Ministry opts for the term *wrath*. I have found *resentment* to be the most common expression.

8. See Jerome Wagner, *Nine Lenses on the World: The Enneagram Perspective* (Evanston, IL: NineLens, 2010), 54.

9. Ian Morgan Cron, *The Story of You: An Enneagram Journey to Becoming Your True Self* (San Francisco: HarperOne, 2021), 72.

10. Rick Warren, *The Purpose Driven Life: What on Earth Am I Here For?* (Grand Rapids: Zondervan, 2002), 127.

11. Dane Ortlund, *Gently and Lowly: The Heart of Christ for Sinners and Sufferers* (Wheaton, IL: Crossway, 2020), 30.

12. The traditional virtue for the One is *serenity*, based on the idea that "everything is perfect just as it is," but I find this carries a notion of obliviousness and passivity that is unhelpful and misaligned. Therefore, I find that *patience* is a more fulfilling and active virtue to practice.

13. Richard Rohr, *Things Hidden: Scripture as Spirituality* (Cincinnati, OH: St. Anthony Messenger, 2008), 25.

14. Donald Miller, *Blue Like Jazz: Nonreligious Thoughts on Christian Spirituality* (Nashville: Nelson, 2012), 86.

15. See AJ Sherrill, *The Enneagram for Spiritual Formation: How Knowing Ourselves Can Make Us More Like Jesus* (Grand Rapids: Brazos, 2020), 68.

16. Sherrill, *Enneagram for Spiritual Formation*, 68.

17. There is an old saying, "The problem with a living sacrifice is that it keeps climbing off the altar." That truth applies here.

18. See Marilyn Vancil, *Self to Lose, Self to Find: Using the Enneagram to Discover Your True, God-Gifted Self* (New York: Convergent, 2020), 61.

Chapter 6: Type Two

1. *The Simpsons*, Season 7, episode 20, "Bart on the Road," dir. Swinton O. Scott III, March 31, 1996.

2. See Don Richard Riso and Russ Hudson, *The Wisdom of the Enneagram: The Complete Guide to Psychological and Spiritual Growth for the Nine Personality Types* (New York: Bantam, 1999), 31.

3. See Riso and Hudson, *Wisdom of the Enneagram*, 32.

4. See CrossPoint Ministry, *The Relational Enneagram Workbook* (Louisville, KY: CrossPoint Ministry, 2021), 20.

5. See Riso and Hudson, *Wisdom of the Enneagram*, 34.

6. Riso and Hudson, *Wisdom of the Enneagram*, 33.

7. See Jerome Wagner, *Nine Lenses on the World: The Enneagram Perspective* (Evanston, IL: NineLens, 2010), 94.

8. C. S. Lewis, *Mere Christianity* (New York: Macmillan, 1952), 109–10.

9. When Jesus talks about the call to deny ourselves, this isn't the type of self-denial he's referring to. He's referring to denying our False Self and our sin. He wants us to lay down our arrogance, our hubris, and our sinful desires and follow him. He wants our True

Selves to walk in both his life and his lifestyle. To bring him our self, we must *have* a self.

10. Wagner, *Nine Lenses on the World*, 54.

11. John Mark Comer, *The Ruthless Elimination of Hurry* (Colorado Springs: WaterBrook, 2019), 130, italics in original.

12. Brennan Manning, *The Furious Longing of God* (Colorado Springs: Cook, 2009), 35.

13. As St. Vincent de Paul has written, "Now humility is nothing but truth, whilst pride is nothing but lying" (quoted in Brigid E. Herman, *Creative Prayer* [New York: Cosimo, 2007], 24).

14. Tom Holladay, *The Relationship Principles of Jesus* (Grand Rapids: Zondervan, 2008), 292.

15. See AJ Sherrill, *The Enneagram for Spiritual Formation: How Knowing Ourselves Can Make Us More Like Jesus* (Grand Rapids: Brazos, 2020), 69–70.

16. See Marilyn Vancil, *Self to Lose, Self to Find: Using the Enneagram to Discover Your True, God-Gifted Self* (New York: Convergent, 2020), 70.

17. I highly recommend Henry Cloud and John Townsend, *Boundaries: When to Say Yes, How to Say No, To Take Control of Your Life*, rev. ed. (1992; repr., Grand Rapids: Zondervan, 2017).

Chapter 7: Type Three

1. See Ian Morgan Cron and Suzanne Stabile, *The Road Back to You: An Enneagram Journey to Self-Discovery* (Downers Grove, IL: InterVarsity, 2016), 136.

2. As Richard Rohr and Andreas Ebert say, "Threes thrown back on themselves are extremely pragmatic: whatever works is true" (*The Enneagram: A Christian Perspective* [New York: Crossroad, 1990], 86).

3. Don Richard Riso and Russ Hudson, *The Wisdom of the Enneagram: The Complete Guide to Psychological and Spiritual Growth for the Nine Personality Types* (New York: Bantam, 1999), 31.

4. Riso and Hudson, *Wisdom of the Enneagram*, 32.

5. See CrossPoint Ministry, *The Relational Enneagram Workbook* (Louisville, KY: CrossPoint Ministry, 2021), 24.

6. Riso and Hudson, *Wisdom of the Enneagram*, 34.

7. See Riso and Hudson, *Wisdom of the Enneagram*, 33.

8. See Jerome Wagner, *Nine Lenses on the World: The Enneagram Perspective* (Evanston, IL: NineLens, 2010), 94.

9. Photo filters is a fitting analogy on another level as well, seeing as some Enneagram teachers believe that *vanity* is actually the deadly sin of the Three.

10. See Wagner, *Nine Lenses on the World*, 54.

11. Rohr and Ebert, *Enneagram*, 237.

12. See Wagner, *Nine Lenses on the World*, 84.

13. See AJ Sherrill, *The Enneagram for Spiritual Formation: How Knowing Ourselves Can Make Us More Like Jesus* (Grand Rapids: Brazos, 2020), 71–72.

14. John Mark Comer, *Live No Lies: Recognize and Resist the Three Enemies That Sabotage Your Peace* (Colorado Springs: WaterBrook, 2021), 46.

15. See Marilyn Vancil, *Self to Lose, Self to Find: Using the Enneagram to Discover Your True, God-Gifted Self* (New York: Convergent, 2020), 78.

Chapter 8: Type Four

1. Rebecca Dennison, "My Rock and My Redeemer," track 1 on *These Things I Remember*, Sojourn Music, April 26, 2005. Used with permission.

2. Don Richard Riso and Russ Hudson, *The Wisdom of the Enneagram: The Complete Guide to Psychological and Spiritual Growth for the Nine Personality Types* (New York: Bantam, 1999), 31.

3. See Riso and Hudson, *Wisdom of the Enneagram*, 32.

4. See CrossPoint Ministry, *The Relational Enneagram Workbook* (Louisville, KY: CrossPoint Ministry, 2021), 28.

5. See Riso and Hudson, *Wisdom of the Enneagram*, 34.

6. See Riso and Hudson, *Wisdom of the Enneagram*, 33.

7. See Jerome Wagner, *Nine Lenses on the World: The Enneagram Perspective* (Evanston, IL: NineLens, 2010), 94.

8. Dorothy L. Sayers, *Letters to a Diminished Church: Passionate Arguments for the Relevance of Christian Doctrine* (Nashville: W Publishing, 2004), 94.

9. See Wagner, *Nine Lenses on the World*, 54.

10. Robert J. Nogosek writes, "Jesus could well be called the patron of misunderstood people" (*Nine Portraits of Jesus: Discovering Jesus through the Enneagram* [Mahwah, NJ: Paulist, 1987], 55).

11. Brennan Manning, *Abba's Child: The Cry of the Heart for Intimate Belonging* (Colorado Springs: NavPress, 1994), 59.

12. See Wagner, *Nine Lenses on the World*, 84.

13. Philip Yancey writes, "It's much easier to act your way into feelings than to feel your way into actions" (*Reaching for the Invisible God: What Can We Expect to Find?* [Grand Rapids: Zondervan, 2000], 86).

14. AJ Sherrill, *The Enneagram for Spiritual Formation: How Knowing Ourselves Can Make Us More Like Jesus* (Grand Rapids: Brazos, 2020), 72–73.

15. See Marilyn Vancil, *Self to Lose, Self to Find: Using the Enneagram to Discover Your True, God-Gifted Self* (New York: Convergent, 2020), 86.

Chapter 9: Type Five

1. Skye Jethani summarizes this approach well: "Silence is the beginning of all worship" (*The Divine Commodity: Discovering a Faith beyond Consumer Christianity* [Grand Rapids: Zondervan, 2009], 33).

2. Don Richard Riso and Russ Hudson, *The Wisdom of the Enneagram: The Complete Guide to Psychological and Spiritual Growth for the Nine Personality Types* (New York: Bantam, 1999), 31.

3. See Riso and Hudson, *Wisdom of the Enneagram*, 32.

4. See CrossPoint Ministry, *The Relational Enneagram Workbook* (Louisville, KY: CrossPoint Ministry, 2021), 32.

5. Riso and Hudson, *Wisdom of the Enneagram*, 34.

6. See Riso and Hudson, *Wisdom of the Enneagram*, 33.

7. The traditional vice is *avarice*—extreme greed for wealth or material gain. I've opted for a more common word, but the outcome is identical.

8. Timothy Keller, *Counterfeit Gods: The Empty Promises of Money, Sex, and Power, and the Only Hope That Matters* (New York: Penguin, 2009), 53.

9. As C. S. Lewis has said, "One doesn't realise in early life that the price of freedom is loneliness. To be happy one must be tied" (Walter Hooper, ed., *The Collected Letters of C. S. Lewis*, vol. 3 [New York: HarperCollins, 2004], 1169).

10. See Jerome Wagner, *Nine Lenses on the World: The Enneagram Perspective* (Evanston, IL: NineLens, 2010), 54.

11. This is based on a quote from the English writer and philosopher G. K. Chesterton: "The worst moment for the atheist is when he is really thankful and has nobody to thank" (The Collected Works of G. K. Chesterton [San Francisco: Ignatius, 1986], 2:75, paraphrasing the poet Dante Gabriel Rossetti).

12. Richard Plass and James Cofield, *The Relational Soul: Moving from*

False Self to Deep Connection (Downers Grove, IL: InterVarsity, 2014), 12.

13. Richard Foster, *Celebration of Discipline: The Path to Spiritual Growth* (San Francisco: HarperSanFrancisco, 1978), 15.

14. Dane Ortlund writes, "When you come to Christ for mercy and love and help in your anguish and perplexity and sinfulness, you are going with the flow of his own deepest wishes, not against them" (*Gentle and Lowly: The Heart of Christ for Sinners and Sufferers* [Wheaton, IL: Crossway, 2020], 38).

15. The traditional virtue for the Five is *nonattachment*, but I find CrossPoint Ministry's proactive term *generosity* to be more helpful (*The Relational Enneagram Workbook* [Louisville, KY: CrossPoint Ministry, 2021], 32).

16. AJ Sherrill, *The Enneagram for Spiritual Formation: How Knowing Ourselves Can Make Us More Like Jesus* (Grand Rapids: Brazos, 2020), 73–74.

17. See Marilyn Vancil, *Self to Lose, Self to Find: Using the Enneagram to Discover Your True, God-Gifted Self* (New York: Convergent, 2020), 95.

18. See Jason Goldman, "Ed Tronick and the 'Still Face Experiment,'" *Scientific American*, October 18, 2010, https://blogs.scientificamerican.com/thoughtful-animal/ed-tronick-and-the-8220-still-face-experiment-8221; see also "Still Face Experiment," YouTube, November 9, 2016, www.youtube.com/watch?v=IeHcsFqK7So.

Chapter 10: Type Six

1. AJ Sherrill, *The Enneagram for Spiritual Formation: How Knowing Ourselves Can Make Us More Like Jesus* (Grand Rapids: Brazos, 2020), 54.

2. Don Richard Riso and Russ Hudson, *The Wisdom of the Enneagram: The Complete Guide to Psychological and Spiritual Growth for the Nine Personality Types* (New York: Bantam, 1999), 31.

3. See Riso and Hudson, *Wisdom of the Enneagram*, 32.

4. See CrossPoint Ministry, *The Relational Enneagram Workbook* (Louisville, KY: CrossPoint Ministry, 2021), 36.

5. Beatrice Chestnut, *The Complete Enneagram: 27 Paths to Greater Self-Knowledge* (Berkeley, CA: She Writes, 2013), 183.

6. See Riso and Hudson, *Wisdom of the Enneagram*, 34.

7. See Riso and Hudson, *Wisdom of the Enneagram*, 33.

8. See Jerome Wagner, *Nine Lenses on the World* (Evanston, IL: NineLens, 2010), 94.

9. See Wagner, *Nine Lenses on the World*, 54.

10. In John 14:27, Jesus also tells us, "Do not let your hearts be troubled and do not be afraid."

11. Karle Wilson Baker, "Three Small Poems: Courage," Poetry Nook, accessed June 24, 2022, www.poetrynook.com/poem /three-small-poems.

12. Catherine Madsen, "The Thin Thread of Conversation: An Interview with Mary Daly," *Cross Currents* 50, no. 3 (Fall 2000), https://catherinemadsen.com/the-thin-thread-of-conversation -an-interview-with-mary-daly.

13. Sherrill, *Enneagram for Spiritual Formation*, 74.

14. I recommend the Bible memory app called "Verses" to help with Scripture memorization. It gamifies the process and makes it a fun and simple experience.

15. See Marilyn Vancil, *Self to Lose, Self to Find: Using the Enneagram to Discover Your True, God-Gifted Self* (New York: Convergent, 2020), 104.

Chapter 11: Type Seven

1. Don Richard Riso and Russ Hudson, *The Wisdom of the Enneagram: The Complete Guide to Psychological and Spiritual Growth for the Nine Personality Types* (New York: Bantam, 1999), 31.

2. See Riso and Hudson, *Wisdom of the Enneagram*, 32.

3. CrossPoint Ministry, *The Relational Enneagram Workbook* (Louisville, KY: CrossPoint Ministry, 2021), 40.

4. Riso and Hudson, *Wisdom of the Enneagram*, 34.

5. See Riso and Hudson, *Wisdom of the Enneagram*, 33

6. See Jerome Wagner, *Nine Lenses on the World* (Evanston, IL: NineLens, 2010), 94.

7. See Wagner, *Nine Lenses on the World*, 54.

8. On the topic of suffering, Tim Keller writes, "Christianity teaches that, contra fatalism, suffering is overwhelming; contra Buddhism, suffering is real; contra karma, suffering is often unfair; but contra secularism, suffering is meaningful. There is a purpose to it, and if faced rightly, it can drive us like a nail deep into the love of God and into more stability and spiritual power than you can imagine"

(*Walking with God through Pain and Suffering* [New York: Penguin, 2013], 30).

9. David Benner, *Surrender to Love: Discovering the Heart of Christian Spirituality* (Downers Grove, IL: InterVarsity, 2003), 14.

10. See Wagner, *Nine Lenses on the World*, 84.

11. You can hear Jonah's story on *The EnneaCast* podcast ("Episode #7: Type 7—The Enthusiast w/ Jonah Sage," July 31, 2018, https://soundcloud.com/ltnenneacast/episode-7).

12. C. S. Lewis wrote, "If you want to get warm you must stand near the fire: if you want to be wet you must get into the water. If you want joy, power, peace, eternal life, you must get close to, or even into, the thing that has them" (*Mere Christianity* [New York: Macmillan, 1960], 153).

13. See AJ Sherrill, *The Enneagram for Spiritual Formation: How Knowing Ourselves Can Make Us More Like Jesus* (Grand Rapids: Brazos, 2020), 76–77.

14. Marilyn Vancil, *Self to Lose, Self to Find: Using the Enneagram to Discover Your True, God-Gifted Self* (New York: Convergent, 2020), 113.

Conclusion

1. See Timothy Keller, "The Real Jesus Part 1: His Teaching," Gospel in Life, September 8, 1996–October 27, 1996, https://gospelinlife.com/downloads/the-real-jesus-part-1-his-teaching.

2. Neal Lozano, *Abba's Heart: Finding Our Way Back to the Father's Delight* (Bloomington, MN: Chosen, 2015), 38.

3. Brennan Manning, *The Furious Longing of God* (Colorado Springs: Cook, 2009), 42–43.

4. Quoted in Manning, *Furious Longing of God*, 77.

5. Tony Evans, *Horizontal Jesus: How Our Relationships with Others Affect Our Experience with God* (Eugene, OR: Harvest House, 2015), 114.

6. John Calvin, *Calvin's Institutes: Abridged Edition*, ed. Donald K. McKim (Louisville, KY: Westminster John Knox, 2001), 1.

ABOUT THE AUTHOR

Jesse Eubanks is a teacher of the Enneagram and host of *The EnneaCast*, a podcast exploring personality and relationships. He is also the founder and executive director of Love Thy Neighborhood, a nonprofit helping people engage Christian discipleship and missions in modern culture. *Relevant* named him one of the top 50 Christian artists and activists who are making an impact on culture in America. Jesse and his wife, Lindsay, have two children and live in Louisville, Kentucky.

More Resources and Next Steps

Visit
https://lovethyneighborhood.org/enneagram/
for more Enneagram resources
and next steps, including:

- "Should Christians Use the Enneagram?" (scan the QR code below to download this free resource)
- *Mapping Your Enneagram Story Workbook*
- Group Discussion Guide
- Podcasts
- Video Courses
- Workshops